The Nuclear Arms Race—

Can We Survive It?

Also by Ann E. Weiss

GOD AND GOVERNMENT:
The Separation of Church and State

TUNE IN, TUNE OUT:
Broadcasting Regulation in the United States

The Nuclear Arms Race —

Can We Survive It?

Ann E. Weiss

Houghton Mifflin Company   Boston

Library of Congress Cataloging in Publication Data

Weiss, Ann E., 1943–
  The nuclear arms race.

  Bibliography: p.
  Includes index.
  Summary: Discusses the history of the post-World
War II arms race and the arguments for and against the
further development and stockpiling of nuclear weapons.
    1. Atomic weapons—Juvenile literature. 2. Arms
race—History—20th century—Juvenile literature.
3. Atomic weapons and disarmament—Juvenile literature.
4. Antinuclear movement—Juvenile literature. [1. Atomic
weapons. 2. Arms race—History—20th century. 3. Atomic
weapons and disarmament. 4. Antinuclear movement]
I. Title.
U264.W44   1983   327.1′74   83-12798
ISBN 0-395-34928-1

Printed in the United States of America

v 10 9 8 7 6 5 4 3

For Margot and Rebecca
and all the rest

Contents

1. BOMBS and a BLAST

Becket is a small town tucked away in the Berkshire Hills of western Massachusetts. It is a rural town of quiet streets, old farmhouses, a white-steepled church on a green lawn — a serene and peaceful town.

Then, one late summer day, the town's serenity and peace were shattered. On September 11, 1982, the BOMBS arrived in Becket. They were met by a BLAST.

Is this the beginning of an imaginary outbreak-of-nuclear-war scenario? No. The BOMBS and BLAST are not imaginary, but real. On that September day, they were part of a protest against United States preparations for nuclear war.

It all started several weeks earlier, at a July Fourth picnic in Burlington, Connecticut. "What would we do if there were a nuclear war?" several of the picnickers wondered aloud. "What would happen to us? Where would we go?" Their hosts, Bill and Diane Tomaney, decided to find out.

For information, the Tomaneys went to the Federal Emergency Management Agency (FEMA). What they learned shocked them. FEMA's emergency civil defense plan said that in the event of nuclear attack, Burlington residents were to travel northward over 60 miles of winding, hilly roads, to Becket. The people of two other Connecticut towns, Beacon Falls and Bethlehem, would also flee to Becket. Altogether, if nuclear war came, the Connecticut refugees would outnumber Becket's 1600 residents by four to one.

How would the people of Becket feel about that? the Tomaneys asked themselves. Where would the refugees stay? How would they find food? Drinking water? Medicines?

There were other questions. Would people be able to travel even as short a distance as 60 miles just before or during a nuclear conflict? Would there be enough gas for autos? Why were Beacon Falls and Bethlehem residents also assigned to Becket? Neither town is particularly close to Burlington. The towns have little in common with each other, or with Becket. Were they simply being grouped together alphabetically? Anyway, why would people from small towns in Connecticut be any safer in a small town in Massachusetts? Becket is only 100 miles from Boston and 115 from New York City. It's less than 150 miles from the United States naval and air stations near Portsmouth, New Hampshire. All three could be prime targets in any nuclear attack.

With such facts and questions in mind, Diane Tomaney and a couple of friends got in touch with surprised Becket officials. Surprised? Definitely. The
people of Becket had never been told they might one
day be called upon to play host to more than 6000
nuclear refugees. The town's 1982 civil defense budget was $50, but so far, not a penny of it had been
spent.

So BOMBS and BLAST were born.

Members of BOMBS — Burlington Organization
for the Movement of Bodies to Safety — began making plans for a mock evacuation to Becket. BLAST —
Becket League for the Assistance of the Scorched and
Terrified — prepared to welcome them. On the day
of the protest, the two groups picnicked together on
the green in front of the Becket church. "It's the best
fun we've had in years," one BLAST organizer re-
marked.

Behind the fun was a serious purpose. Members of
BOMBS and BLAST hoped to dramatize some of the
problems they believed existed in FEMA's nuclear
civil defense program.

Nuclear civil defense planning is nonsensical, they
think. "Just ludicrous" is the way one Becket official
described it. Just as nonsensical as the idea of nuclear civil defense, they believe, is the idea that there
could ever be any cause that would justify having a
nuclear war in the first place.

Such a war could devastate large areas of the world. It could kill millions — perhaps hundreds of millions — of people. It would poison the earth with deadly, invisible, nuclear radiation.

Or it could destroy our planet, with all its peoples, all their history, all their hopes and dreams and aspirations, completely and forever.

Is such destruction possible? A 1982 United States Department of Defense report showed that the United States possessed a total of 9000 long-range nuclear warheads. Experts estimate that altogether these warheads contained the equivalent explosive power of about 4000 megatons — 4,000,000,000 tons — of TNT. (Other estimates place the number of American weapons, and their explosive force, somewhat higher or lower.)

It is estimated that the Soviet Union, the world's other nuclear superpower, owned fewer long-range warheads than the United States — perhaps about 7000 of them. But their combined explosive force was greater. It added up to the equivalent of 7000 megatons of TNT. Together, the United States and the Soviet Union have enough nuclear weapons to kill all the people in the world — all 4.5 billion of them — several times over. Four other nations, Great Britain, France, China, and India, also have nuclear weapons, although not nearly as many as either the Soviet Union or the United States.

Even using just one average-sized nuclear weapon — a one-megaton bomb — could mean vast destruction. According to the United States Office of Technology Assessment, such a weapon, dropped on Detroit, would kill over 215,000 people and injure twice as many more. At the center of the blast — ground zero — only a crater, 1000 feet wide and 200 feet deep, would remain. For nearly two miles in every direction, not a single structure would be left standing. For miles beyond that, most homes and smaller buildings would be destroyed or badly damaged.

The heat at the center of a nuclear explosion can reach 10 million degrees Fahrenheit. This heat, and the tremendous updraft it created, could start a firestorm of enormously concentrated heat and ferocity. Or it could ignite a series of conflagrations that would sweep across the devastated city. Overhead would hang a dense, mushroom-shaped cloud of dust and debris. This cloud would give off the deadly radiation that accompanies any nuclear reaction. This intense radiation would cause severe burns, burns that would kill thousands of men, women, and children who survived the actual blast.

Caught by the winds of the atmosphere, the radioactive particles would quickly spread. Many would fall out toward the earth, causing radiation sickness, cancers, and other illnesses to people in its path. How far the nuclear fallout would reach — whether over hundreds or thousands of miles, and in which direction — would depend upon wind and weather conditions and upon whether the weapon was exploded on the ground or in the air. In the Detroit area itself, radiation levels would remain dangerously high for tens, if not hundreds, of years.

Just one "average" nuclear weapon could do all this. The United States and the Soviet Union own thousands of "average" weapons. Both also own some weapons that are even more powerful.

Yet neither nation is satisfied. Each is working frantically to develop new, more powerful, more accurate nuclear weapons. The result is a nuclear arms race that grows year by year, with no sign of slowing down.

Slowing down the arms race is what BOMBS and BLAST are all about. These groups are not alone. Around the country, people in hundreds of antinuclear groups are speaking and acting against the arms race and the threat of nuclear war. This antinuclear activity is not new. It started nearly four decades ago, and was particularly widespread in the 1950s. After that, it died down — until now.

Antinuclear activity goes beyond the United States. There are antinuclear movements all over Western Europe, in Canada, Japan, Australia, and Latin

America. Even the tiny islands of the South Pacific Ocean have seen antinuclear activity.

The ultimate aim of many in the antinuclear movement is to get rid of all nuclear weapons, everywhere in the world. For others in the movement, the goal is different — strict arms control. Nuclear weapons are here to stay, these people believe, and nations must agree to manage their arsenals to avoid an ever-growing arms race and the possibility of nuclear war. But leaders of the movement know that before they can even hope to accomplish either disarmament or true arms control, they must educate people about nuclear weapons and nuclear war. They must make them realize just how fierce — and how dangerous — the nuclear arms race is.

It was to educate people and to call world attention to their cause that more than two million antinuclear activists marched through the streets of various cities of Europe during the fall of 1981. Americans marched for the same purpose the next spring. On Saturday, June 12, 1982, a crowd of more than half a million men, women, and children walked from the United Nations headquarters in New York City uptown to Central Park. There they listened to a program of antinuclear songs and speeches. The New York City march was the largest single demonstration ever held in the United States.

That same weekend in New York, ten thousand people attended a special service at the city's Cathedral of St. John the Divine. Spilling out of the church and into the streets, the worshipers prayed for an end to the arms race. They heard readings from the holy works of Christianity, Judaism, Buddhism, Hinduism, Islam, and the Hopi Indians.

It was fitting that the service reflected many nations and many faiths. Jew or Christian, Hindu or Buddhist, German or American or Russian or Latin American — the issue of the nuclear arms race unites us all. That race may be making nuclear war more and more likely. If nuclear war does come, it will not affect the people of just one or two cities or countries. It will change the life of every person in the world.

Can nuclear war be avoided? The arms race stopped? What can the antinuclear movement really hope to accomplish?

2. The First Bomb

Even before the nuclear arms race really began, a few men and women were trying to stop it. Among them were some of the very people who had helped start it in the first place.

One such person was Albert Einstein. Einstein was born in 1879, in Germany. During the early 1900s, while he was living and working in Switzerland, Einstein developed his famous formula: $E = mc^2$.

According to this formula, the amount of Energy in any bit of matter equals the mass (weight) of that matter times the speed of light (c), squared (multiplied times itself).

What does that mean? Take the atom — the smallest unit of an element. At the heart, or core, of each atom is its nucleus. Locked up inside that nucleus is an amount of energy equal to the mass of the atom times the speed of light, times itself.

The mass of an individual atom is tiny. But the speed of light is 186,000 miles per second. Multiplied by itself, that comes to an enormous number.

Using his formula, Einstein predicted that suddenly releasing the nuclear energy from just one ounce of matter could produce a blast equal to the explosion of a million tons of TNT. Or, if the energy were released slowly, it might be used to generate a steady electrical current. The energy could be released by splitting apart the nucleus of every atom in the ounce of matter.

But at the beginning of the twentieth century, no one knew how to do that. It was two decades before scientists learned to split — fission — the atom. Even then, they were only able to split a few atoms at a time, nowhere near enough to release any useful amount of energy. Again and again, experimenters started fissioning atoms only to have the reaction slow down and stop.

It was not until the late 1930s that two scientists, Leo Szilard and Enrico Fermi, thought of a method to keep the reaction going. On March 3, 1939, an experiment proved that their method would work. Soon, a nuclear chain reaction — a fission reaction that sustains itself — would be possible.

The two scientists performed their successful experiment at Columbia University in New York City. Szilard, who was Hungarian, and Fermi, an Italian, had come to the United States to escape the dictatorships of Adolf Hitler and Benito Mussolini.

Szilard and Fermi were delighted by their success — but worried, too. If they had made such progress, so could scientists in Europe, especially in Germany, where nuclear research had been going on for years. With that success (which, they later learned, German scientists *had* already had), might come the ability to build a nuclear bomb. What, Szilard and Fermi wondered, would a person like Hitler, a man bent on world conquest, do with such a weapon? War seemed to be about to break out in Europe. Armed with nuclear weapons, Hitler could win an easy victory there and then move on to threaten the United States.

As a matter of fact, Hitler never came close to having a nuclear bomb. He refused to listen to scientists who claimed one could be built, and ordered them to concentrate on other weapons instead. In addition, by persecuting Germany's most brilliant scientists, such as Einstein, Hitler deprived the country of the very men and women who might have solved the problems remaining in the way of developing a nuclear bomb. So Szilard and Fermi were reacting to a threat that did not exist, although they could not have known that.

The fearful scientists took their concerns to Einstein. He, too, had fled the European dictatorships; he was living and working at Princeton University, in New Jersey. In August 1939, just a month before World War II began, Einstein sent a letter to President Franklin D. Roosevelt. In it, he warned that Germany might soon be able to build nuclear bombs. He advised the president to concentrate American efforts on producing these weapons before Germany could.

That is just what Roosevelt decided to do. A specially equipped laboratory was set up at the University of Chicago, and Fermi moved there to continue his experiments. Other scientists were appointed as his assistants. Large amounts of uranium, the "fuel" for nuclear chain reactions, were shipped to Chicago.

At first, the work went slowly. Then, on December 7, 1941, Japanese planes attacked the U.S. naval fleet at Pearl Harbor, Hawaii. Within days, the United States was at war with both Germany and Italy, as well as with Japan. Suddenly, becoming the first nation to develop nuclear weapons seemed vital.

In August 1942, the job of supervising nuclear research was handed over to the United States Army. Under a code name, the Manhattan Project, the work was given top priority in various parts of the country. The work soon showed results.

In Oak Ridge, Tennessee, scientists labored to refine uranium ore into its purest — and therefore most fissionable — state. In Hanford, Washington, huge nuclear reactors produced another highly fissionable material — plutonium. In Chicago, Fermi and others produced the first nuclear chain reaction. And in the desert town of Los Alamos, New Mexico, a team of nuclear physicists gathered to design a workable nuclear bomb. The Los Alamos group was headed by a scientist from the University of California, J. Robert Oppenheimer.

Oppenheimer was another person who helped start the nuclear arms race — and then tried to stop it. Under his direction, the Los Alamos scientists designed and built three nuclear bombs. The first, code-named Trinity, was scheduled to be tested on July 16, 1945, at Alamogordo, New Mexico.

Before the test, some of the Los Alamos scientists placed friendly bets on how powerful the Trinity explosion would be. The bets ranged from a low of 300 tons of TNT to a high of 45,000 tons, but the scientists' official prediction was 5000 tons.

After the test, Fermi did some rapid calculations. Trinity's blast, he announced, had equaled approximately 20,000 tons of TNT.

Soberly, Oppenheimer looked out over the test site, where a giant mushroom cloud of fire, smoke, steam, dust, and debris was billowing upward. He had suddenly realized just how destructive this weapon — this weapon he had worked so hard to create — was going to be. "I am become death," he said softly, quoting from the holy writings of the Hindu religion. "I am become death, the shatterer of worlds."

But Trinity was only a test. Now the question was:

Should the United States use its other nuclear weapons to shatter actual worlds? Should it drop nuclear bombs on Japan?

Passionately, the Los Alamos scientists debated the question. So did the army officers who had directed the Manhattan Project. So did President Harry S Truman, who had assumed office in April after President Roosevelt's sudden death, and his closest White House advisers.

There were strong arguments against using the bombs. Germany had already surrendered, so the United States was free to concentrate on defeating Japan with conventional (nonnuclear) weapons. What's more, even those who built Trinity were appalled by its enormous destructiveness. How could America be responsible for unleashing such a dreadful weapon against hundreds of thousands of men, women, and children?

Some who opposed using the bomb on Japan directly suggested alternatives. One was detonating a weapon so high in the air that it would do little damage on the ground. Another was to invite Japanese military and political leaders to view an atom bomb test. Either demonstration would be a powerful argument in favor of immediate Japanese surrender, they said.

Others were not so sure. What if the demonstration failed? Nuclear weapons were still experimental, and the scientists at Los Alamos might well have constructed a dud. Then the Japanese would think American talk about its powerful new weapon was just a bluff. They would fight on more fiercely than ever, prolonging the war for months.

Prolonging the war could be disastrous for the United States, the argument continued. It might mean this country would have to invade the Japanese islands. That could result in the loss of a million or more American troops.

Another argument in favor of using the bombs involved the Soviet Union. During the war, the Soviet Union and the United States had been allies. But with peace in sight, tensions were building between the two nations. Already, the Soviets had taken over several of the countries of Eastern Europe. Now they appeared eager to advance across the Pacific Ocean and seize even more territory. American officials did not want that to happen. Ending the war at once, they believed, was the only way to stop the Soviets in the Pacific.

In the end, as everyone knows, those who wanted to use the bombs won the argument. On August 6, 1945, a nuclear bomb fueled with uranium was dropped on the Japanese city of Hiroshima. It had the explosive force of 20,000 tons of TNT and killed more than 100,000 people outright. Thousands more died in the next weeks and months. Even now, in the

1980s, men and women who survived the blast are dying from diseases caused by the bomb's nuclear radiation.

Three days after the Hiroshima bombing, the United States dropped a plutonium-fueled bomb on Nagasaki. Again, a single weapon killed and injured over 70,000 people. On August 14, Japan surrendered.

The war was over, but America's nuclear dilemma had barely begun. Even though peace had come, government labs and research stations continued to turn out nuclear weapons. Now, however, people were beginning to raise questions — moral questions — about nuclear weapons.

J. Robert Oppenheimer, watching newsreels of Nagasaki and Hiroshima, was horrified by pictures of terribly burned children, of people dying in an agony of radiation poisoning, of shadows of the dead, forever burned into the pavement by the searing heat of the blasts.

Albert Einstein was horrified, too. His formula, $E = mc^2$, had helped to form the basis of nuclear physics. His letter to President Roosevelt had helped prompt the race to build nuclear weapons. Yet all his life, Einstein had supported the cause of world peace. Now he was determined to work for that cause through a newly formed international organization, the United Nations.

Others hoped to use the UN to ensure that there would never be another nuclear war. In November 1945, President Truman announced the goal of "the elimination from national armaments of atomic weapons." The next month, he sent his secretary of state, James F. Byrnes, to the Soviet Union. Part of Byrnes's mission was to persuade Soviet leaders to agree to UN control of nuclear energy. That included nuclear energy for peaceful civilian purposes, as well as for military uses.

Although the Soviets showed little interest in the American proposal, Truman and his advisers pursued it. They asked a number of scientists, including Oppenheimer, to report on how the UN might take over responsibility for nuclear matters.

By March 1946, the report was ready. It called for setting up an International Atomic Development Authority (IADA). The IADA would be the only organization in the world with the right to gather nuclear raw materials, such as uranium. It would carry out all research on peaceful uses of nuclear energy — in medicine and industry, and for generating electrical power. The IADA would also have the authority to license nuclear power plants around the world.

Finally, the IADA would act as a "nuclear police force." Its agents would carry out regular inspections to make sure that no nation was secretly building nuclear weapons. After the IADA was set up and functioning, the report concluded, the United States would turn all its nuclear weapons over to it.

Truman and his advisers approved the report and sent it on to the United States representative to the UN Atomic Energy Commission, Bernard Baruch. After studying it, Baruch made one major change. He added a clause that would give the IADA the power to punish any country that did try to produce nuclear weapons.

In June, Baruch presented the report, now known as the Baruch Plan, to the UN. The Baruch Plan was the most radical disarmament plan — the only nuclear disarmament plan — ever offered by the United States. It called for unilateral (one-sided) nuclear disarmament. If it had been adopted, the nuclear arms race might have ended almost before it began.

That did not happen. The Soviet Union would not agree to the Baruch Plan.

Why not? The plan made no demands on the Soviet Union. Only the United States had to give up nuclear weapons because only the United States owned nuclear weapons. The Soviet Union had much larger conventional forces than the United States did in 1946, and the Baruch Plan left those forces untouched.

Nevertheless, the Soviet Union strongly objected to parts of the plan. One objection had to do with inspections. Soviet leaders did not want foreigners going into their plants and factories to look for evidence of illegal activity. They feared that would give other nations a chance to spy on Soviet industry. They were also afraid it would reveal to the world how badly the Soviet Union had been damaged during World War II and how weak it still was.

Furthermore, the Soviets pointed out — quite correctly — that inspection was a whole new idea in international relations. Always before, when countries signed a weapons agreement, they simply trusted each other to abide by it. Why change the rules now? the Soviets demanded.

Soviet leaders had other objections. For example, they doubted that the IADA would act fairly to all nations. The United States was the only nation that understood the secrets of the atom. So United States scientists·would naturally dominate the IADA. Would they really share their nuclear secrets with the Soviet Union?

And what about the provision that the United States would turn over its nuclear weapons as soon as the IADA was in full operation? Who would decide what "full operation" meant? Obviously, it would be the United States government. What if American leaders just kept delaying and delaying? Then the United States would have a growing nuclear arsenal, while the Soviets would never have a chance to develop nuclear weapons at all.

Finally, Soviet leaders objected to the idea of punishing nations that did build nuclear weapons. During the UN debate on the Baruch Plan, it became clear what the American idea of punishment was. The United States would turn over its nuclear weapons to the IADA. Then those weapons would be used against any nation found to be producing its own nuclear bombs.

From the Soviet point of view, the threat was clear. America had nuclear weapons. America was in a position to keep all nuclear secrets from the Soviet Union. If the Soviets tried to discover those secrets on its own, the IADA, directed by the United States, would launch a nuclear attack against the Soviet Union. To Soviet leaders, the Baruch Plan seemed a plot to allow the United States to dominate the rest of the world through its nuclear weapons.

Soviet leaders may have been wrong in their suspicions. But it was not unreasonable that they had such suspicions. What was unreasonable — and tragic — was that the Soviets refused even to discuss the Baruch Plan.

Five days after the plan was made public, Soviet leaders rejected it. Instead, they called on the United States to get rid of all its nuclear arms within three months, and to stop building more. In return, the Soviet Union would promise not to try to develop nuclear weapons. There would be no inspections, and no punishment for a nation that did go ahead with a nuclear weapons program.

The United States rejected the Soviet plan as abruptly as the Soviets had rejected the Baruch Plan. American leaders and their scientific advisers knew that a nuclear disarmament plan would be meaningless without some way of keeping tabs on nuclear developments around the world.

Nuclear weapons are not like conventional armaments. To build tanks, aircraft, and artillery requires large factories and many workers. Building nuclear weapons requires less space and a smaller work force. It would not be impossible for a nation to build nuclear weapons in secret and to hide what it was doing from the outside world. After all, that was exactly what the scientists of the Manhattan Project had done. American leaders flatly refused to consider any nuclear disarmament plan that did not include a provision for inspections.

The American rejection probably came as no surprise to the Soviets. Many historians conclude that Soviet leaders never really expected the United States to consider their proposal. They had offered it largely in order to divert world attention from their own rejection of the Baruch Plan. The Soviets may also have hoped that the quick United States rejection would put America in a bad light. Their "offer" was little more than a propaganda ploy. Such tactics have been repeated, by the United States as well as by the Soviet Union, many times in the years since 1946.

So the first nuclear arms negotiations were stale-mated. Over the next eight years, the United States stuck to the Baruch Plan. The Soviet Union continued to reject it. No progress was made on disarmament. But the nuclear arms race flourished, and so did tensions between the Soviet Union and the United States.

3.   From Cold War to SALT

The United States dropped nuclear bombs on Japan partly because it distrusted the Soviet Union. The Soviet Union turned down the Baruch Plan partly because it was suspicious of the United States. That was just the beginning. Over the next years, suspicion and distrust grew between the two nations. It was the time of the "cold war."

The cold war got its name because it was not a "hot," or fighting, war. It was a time of fear and hostility, though not of killing.

Each side seemed to have reason to mistrust the other. The United States was dismayed by Soviet takeovers in Eastern Europe, and by threatened takeovers elsewhere.

The United States contributed to the tension as well. Once Germany was defeated, some American politicans and military men suggested going ahead and invading the Soviet Union while it was still weakened by war. Although the United States never

did this, Soviet leaders were well aware that the idea
had been suggested.

Time passed, and the cold war became more intense. The Soviet Union seemed set to grab more and
more lands. Soviet leaders bragged that they would
one day triumph over the United States.

The United States took the Soviet threats seriously.
In 1949, this country, along with Canada, Iceland,
and nine Western European nations, agreed to form
the North Atlantic Treaty Organization (NATO).
NATO was — and still is — a military alliance
against the Soviet Union. NATO countries agreed to
look upon a Soviet attack on any one of them as an
attack on all. If the Soviet Union invaded West Germany, or Norway, or any other NATO nation, then
all the members of NATO, including the United
States, would strike back. NATO has its own army,
to which the United States currently contributes more
than 300,000 troops.

NATO made the Soviets uneasy. Their uneasiness
increased in 1954. That year, the United States and
its Western European allies decided to allow West
Germany to rebuild its army, navy, and air force.
The Soviet Union, which had lost more than 20 million people at the hands of the German armed forces
during World War II, was alarmed by the idea of a
rearmed Germany. It responded by setting up the
Warsaw Pact.

The Warsaw Pact, the Soviet answer to NATO, is an alliance between the Soviet Union and the Communist nations of Eastern Europe. By the mid-1950s, NATO and Warsaw Pact forces were facing each other across Europe, armed and prepared to fight.

The Soviet Union and the United States were preparing for war in other ways. Each was trying to get ahead of the other in nuclear armaments.

To begin with, the United States had a tremendous advantage. It was the only nuclear nation. But Soviet scientists were working hard to catch up, and in 1949, they exploded their first nuclear bomb.

American leaders were dismayed. Throughout the fall of 1949, President Truman met with scientific and military experts to discuss how the United States should respond. The central issue was whether or not the United States should try to build a new kind of weapon, a thermonuclear weapon, or "Super Bomb."

A thermonuclear bomb, scientists informed Truman and his military advisers, would be very different from the bombs that destroyed Hiroshima and Nagasaki. Those earlier weapons were fission bombs. They produced their explosions when atoms of a heavy metal like uranium or plutonium were split apart.

The thermonuclear weapon, on the other hand, would work by fusion. Its explosion would be caused by the fusion, or coming together, of the nuclei of atoms of a very light material, hydrogen. Thus the name hydrogen bomb, or H-bomb, in contrast to the A-bomb, the atomic bomb. Fusion produces a far more powerful explosion than fission. In fact, it takes a fission explosion just to get the fusion reaction going. Even a small fusion weapon would create a blast many times more powerful and devastating than the blasts at Hiroshima and Nagasaki.

One scientist who argued in favor of the H-bomb was Edward Teller, who had worked on the Manhattan Project at Los Alamos. Teller maintained that having the H-bomb would put the United States way ahead of the Soviet Union in the nuclear arms race. It would make America safer, better able to defend itself against its cold-war enemy, he said.

J. Robert Oppenheimer opposed building the H-bomb. He predicted that if the United States built a hydrogen bomb, the Soviet Union would quickly do the same. The United States would not come out ahead, but the arms race would heat up. Oppenheimer argued that the United States ought to follow a different path, and hold back on the H-bomb. That might inspire the Soviets to hold back, too.

Oppenheimer's argument failed to convince the president. In January 1950, Truman told American scientists to begin work on the hydrogen bomb.

The work was carried out in secret, just as work on the Manhattan Project had been. President Truman's decision to build the H-bomb was made in secret, too. Only a few scientists, military officers, and leaders of Congress took part in the debate. The American people knew nothing of what was going on. They had no chance to express an opinion for or against plunging ahead with the arms race.

What if Truman's decision had been different? Was Oppenheimer right? If the United States had not gone ahead with the H-bomb, would the Soviet Union have done so? No one can say for sure. But Oppenheimer was correct in the other part of his prediction. The United States exploded a hydrogen device in 1952. The Soviet Union exploded one in 1953.

Now the nuclear arms race was in full swing. The United States and the Soviet Union were rapidly building up their stockpiles of fission and fusion bombs. Both also developed better, more efficient ways of getting nuclear weapons to their targets.

One new delivery system was the long-range bomber. Long-range bombers are jet planes with a flying range great enough that each country can attack the other directly, rather than from bases in Europe or the Far East. Even more significant, scientists in both countries were working on ballistic missile systems.

Up to this time, nuclear weapons had been bombs. They were designed to be dropped from planes. A ballistic missile is different. It consists of a rocket armed with a nuclear weapon. The rocket is aimed and fired. It delivers its deadly "payload" directly to its target. A powerful enough rocket can carry a nuclear warhead over 3000 miles — across an entire ocean or continent. Hence its name: intercontinental ballistic missile (ICBM).

The Soviet Union tested an ICBM in August 1957. Two months later, that success was followed by another — the Soviet launching of the world's first artificial satellite. The Soviets called it Sputnik.

The Soviet advances left Americans shaken. No longer was the United States safe from attack, protected by two great oceans. Thanks to its ICBMs and its long-range bombers, the Soviet Union could attack any American military base directly. Worse still, the Soviets could arm a Sputnik-like satellite with nuclear weapons and orbit it across the United States. It would pose a constant threat to every American town, city, or military installation under its path.

Worried United States officials lost no time. Warning of a "bomber gap" — a gap that they believed meant the Soviet Union had more long-range bombers than the United States — they announced a crash program to build more planes. By 1958, the United States had five times as many long-range bombers as the Soviet Union. That huge imbalance was proof, a number of people charged, that the bomber gap had never actually existed.

Next, United States concern shifted to a "missile gap." During the presidential election campaign of 1960, Democratic candidate John F. Kennedy charged that the Soviet Union had more ICBMs than the United States did. If he were elected, Kennedy promised, he would see to it that the United States caught up.

Kennedy was elected, and the United States began a massive missile-building program. As it turned out, the missile gap was no more real than the bomber gap of a few years before. In 1967, President Lyndon Johnson revealed that fact casually to friends at a party. Johnson, who was Kennedy's vice president, became president when Kennedy was assassinated in 1963. Now, four years later, he admitted that he and other Democrats had been wrong about Soviet missile strength in 1960. "It turns out," he said, "our guesses were way off. We were doing things we didn't need to do. We were building things we didn't need to build. We were harboring fears we didn't need to harbor."

But needed or not, the ICBMs were built.

New United States missiles were stationed in Europe, too, at the beginning of the 1960s. Intermediate-range ballistic missiles (IRBMs), with a range of up to 1200 miles, were placed in such NATO countries as Turkey, West Germany, Italy, and Britain. The United States also developed the SLBM — submarine-launched ballistic missile — and soon its nuclear-armed subs were patrolling the oceans of the world. The Soviet Union, of course, was working on its own IRBM and SLBM programs.

The United States and the Soviet Union were interested in quality, as well as quantity, of weapons. Both were as determined to improve weapon accuracy and deadliness as to build up large stockpiles. Before long, ballistic missiles in both countries were being equipped with Multiple Reentry Vehicles (MRVs). A MRVed missile has not one but several nuclear warheads. Fired at a target, the warheads fall to earth at different points along the flight path. Each lands separately, producing its own nuclear blast. A further refinement is the Multiple Independently Targetable Reentry Vehicle (MIRV). In a MIRVed missile, each nuclear warhead can be aimed at a specific individual target.

As soon as the United States and the Soviet Union had their sophisticated ballistic missile systems in place, each began working on antiballistic missiles (ABMs). ABMs are defense systems. They are designed to protect a nation against an ICBM attack. ABM systems have never been thoroughly tested, but in theory, they could intercept and destroy an enemy's missiles before those missiles could do any damage.

During the 1960s, both countries were working on plans to place ABMs around their biggest cities and most important military bases. But before either could get an ABM system in place, things began to change. The Soviet Union and the United States were talking seriously to each other about ways to control the arms race.

Actually, the talking had begun some years earlier. Back in the mid-1950s, Soviet leaders started having second thoughts about the issue of nuclear inspections. It was the idea of international inspection, aimed at uncovering illegal nuclear research, that had been largely responsible for Soviet rejection of the Baruch Plan in 1946.

But during the eight years that followed that rejection, the Soviets developed their own nuclear weapons program. They knew a lot more about nuclear science now, and they realized how easy it would be for a nation to construct nuclear bombs in secret. For the first time, they agreed that any nuclear disarmament plan would have to include some provision for making sure neither side cheated. It looked as if the Baruch Plan finally had a chance.

As it turned out, it did not. As soon as the Soviets showed signs of interest in the plan, the United States withdrew it.

Why? Like the Soviet Union, the United States had

had second thoughts about nuclear weapons. By the mid-1950s, this country no longer wanted nuclear disarmament.

One reason for this had to do with cold-war tensions. The United States did not trust the Soviet Union to stick to its side of any bargain.

Another reason concerned changing American ideas about the best way to prevent a nuclear war. Immediately after World War II, U.S. leaders thought disarmament was the best way. No nuclear weapons would mean no nuclear war, they said. But since then, they had come up with a new theory: deterrence.

According to this theory, a country can avoid nuclear war by being armed heavily enough that no other country would dare attack it. Country A makes it clear to Country B that if B attacks A, A will respond with a counterattack that will utterly destroy B, and incinerate millions of its citizens. That deters — scares off — Country B. Country B is so anxious to avoid such devastation that it does everything in its power to avoid war.

What about Country A, though? Might it start a war?

No, say the supporters of deterrence, provided Countries A and B have roughly the same number of nuclear weapons. This weapons equality is called "parity."

Parity is essential to the theory of deterrence. If

Country A has many more weapons than Country B, A might be tempted to launch a first strike and conquer B. Or B might become so worried about such an attack by A that it would attack A first, in spite of having fewer weapons. This "pre-emptive" first strike would take A by surprise. B might be able to wipe out so many of A's weapons that A could not retaliate. So in a way, it might be as dangerous for Country A to have too *many* nuclear weapons as it would be to have too *few!*

Parity's role is to provide for Mutual Assured Destruction. Mutual Assured Destruction means exactly what it says. It means that if nuclear war begins, each side will continue to attack until both sides are totally destroyed.

But Mutual Assured Destruction will not work unless each country has enough nuclear weapons to survive an attack and to retaliate with a strike of its own. And both A and B must accept that. "The threatened retaliation," one American arms expert has explained, "must be the killing of a major fraction of the Soviet population; moreover, the same ability to kill our own population must be guaranteed the Soviet government."

In other words, for Mutual Assured Destruction to work, each nation must be willing to become an accomplice in the destruction of its own people. Mutual Assured Destruction means that if a nuclear war starts, it will be a war without winners — perhaps without survivors.

That does not sound very sensible. It's the reason critics of the theory refer to it as MAD.

But people who believe in MAD say that it is its very lack of sense that makes the theory work. Neither Country A nor Country B will be willing to risk total annihilation. So each will do all it can to avoid starting a nuclear war.

Good theories or bad, MAD and deterrence are what the Soviet Union and the United States depend upon to prevent nuclear war. But in order for such theories to work, many experts believe, the two sides must maintain parity. They must not let either side get way ahead of the other. They must keep the nuclear arms race under control.

Controlling the arms race takes effort. It takes cooperation. It takes careful discussions about missile systems, stockpile levels, and new weapons development. It takes hours and hours of thoughtful negotiations. And hours of negotiations are just what the Soviet Union and the United States have engaged in since the 1950s when they gave up trying to achieve disarmament and settled for deterrence instead.

One early subject for negotiation was the matter of pollution from nuclear weapons testing. By the 1950s, scientists from many nations were reporting increased levels of strontium 90 in milk and other dairy products. Chemically, strontium 90 resembles calcium, and like calcium, it is concentrated in milk. Strontium 90 is one of the radioactive products given off in a nuclear reaction. It was part of the nuclear fallout that was spreading around the world. Before long, strontium 90 was also showing up in the teeth and bones of children who drank the contaminated milk.

From the American Southwest, where much nuclear testing was done, came word of the mysterious deaths of hundreds of sheep. Although local farmers and ranchers blamed the deaths on the testing, the United States government denied any link between the two. (That link has since been proven beyond any reasonable doubt.)

There was never any question, however, of the link between the 1954 test of a United States H-bomb in the Pacific Ocean and the death of a Japanese fisherman. The test was conducted at the Bikini Atoll in the South Pacific. Winds carried the radioactive mushroom cloud up and out over the sea. Under its path was a small Japanese fishing vessel, the *Lucky Dragon*. As the cloud passed overhead, deadly radioactive dust and gases fell out upon the *Lucky Dragon* and its crew. All those aboard suffered radiation poisoning. One died.

The fisherman's death galvanized worldwide public opinion. "Ban the bomb!" became the cry of a growing antinuclear movement in Europe and America. In the United States, Albert Einstein and other scientists and scholars called on nations to end the production of nuclear weapons and to find other ways than war to settle their differences. The Soviet Union and the United States began discussing a treaty to ban nuclear weapons testing.

The two countries did not reach an agreement for nearly a decade. Even then, what they agreed to was only a partial ban.

The Partial Test Ban Treaty was signed in 1963. It forbids nuclear testing in the atmosphere, in outer space, and in the ocean, but it says nothing about tests carried out far below the earth's surface. The United States and the Soviet Union continue to test their weapons underground. What's more, some nations that test nuclear weapons refused to sign the treaty. France refused, and so did the People's Republic of China. China still tests in the atmosphere, although France stopped doing so in 1975.

Once American and Soviet negotiators signed the Partial Test Ban Treaty, the treaty went to the United States Senate for ratification. Under the Constitution, two-thirds of the members of the Senate must approve any treaty before it becomes binding on the United States. The Senate did vote in favor of the treaty, 80 to 19.

The United States and the Soviet Union have

reached other arms-control agreements over the years. In 1962, the Soviets agreed to dismantle missile launching sites in Cuba. Later, the United States withdrew IRBMs from Europe.

In 1967, the two nations signed the Outer Space Treaty, which bans the placing of nuclear weapons of mass destruction in space. Five years later, the Sea Bed Treaty went into effect. This forbids the putting of nuclear weapons on the ocean floor.

In 1968, the Soviet Union and the United States finished negotiating a major agreement, the Non-Proliferation Treaty (NPT). The NPT has been signed by more than 110 countries. It is designed to keep nuclear weapons from getting into the hands of more and more nations. Under its terms, nations that do not already have nuclear weapons promise not to try to develop them. In return, those nations get help from countries like the United States and the Soviet Union in setting up nuclear plants for peaceful uses, such as the production of electrical energy.

For the Soviet Union and the United States, the NPT was an important step. Leaders of both countries wanted to prevent new nations from joining the "nuclear club." They knew that the more nations that have nuclear weapons, the less well deterrence will work, and the more likely a nuclear war will become. However, the NPT has been far from a complete success. It does not affect countries such as

Britain, China, and France, which already had nuclear weapons when it was signed. It did not keep India from exploding its first nuclear weapon in 1974. It is not keeping Argentina, South Africa, and Pakistan, none of which has signed the treaty, from pushing ahead with their own nuclear weapons programs.

In 1969, the United States and the Soviet Union began a new set of negotiations, the Strategic Arms Limitations Talks (SALT). The aim of these negotiations was to set limits on strategic weapons — long-range weapons and delivery systems. The two sides also talked about limits on antiballistic missile systems. They did not discuss tactical nuclear weapons. Tactical weapons have only a short range. They are designed to be used on the battlefield.

The first round of the Strategic Arms Limitations Talks lasted for three years. In 1972, the Soviet Union and the United States announced that they had reached an agreement. Both sides would limit ABM development. Each country would be permitted to place 100 ABMs around its capital and 100 around one other city or military base. But the two ABM sites would have to be in separate parts of the country — far enough apart that they could not become the start of an ABM network.

The idea behind this provision was simple. Neither side really wanted an ABM system. Both feared ABM networks might be destabilizing — might upset deterrence. If Country A had a strong ABM system, and B did not, A might feel it could safely attack B and then survive B's counterattack. Or, B might launch a pre-emptive surprise attack against an enemy with a strong ABM system. A third possibility is that if both A and B had nationwide ABM networks, the two might decide that nuclear war was no more dangerous than conventional war. The deterrent would be gone.

So the United States and the Soviet Union agreed to ABM limits. They also agreed to limit the numbers of ICBMs and SLBMs each side could own. However, they set those limits high — much higher than anything either side already had in 1972.

The SALT agreement did nothing to reduce nuclear arsenals. Rather, it allowed those arsenals to grow. SALT was really an agreement to continue the arms race, with some new rules. It was not an agreement to try to stop the race. The Senate approved SALT by a vote of 88 to 2.

As soon as the SALT treaty became official, the Soviet Union and the United States began a new round of talks — SALT II. These talks went on for seven years. By 1979, leaders of the two nations had agreed to set further limits on some ICBM systems, to find better ways to make sure both countries were complying with SALT I, and to exchange certain information about the results of nuclear research. In

1979, United States President Jimmy Carter and Soviet President Leonid Brezhnev signed SALT II. Carter sent the treaty to the Senate.

Before the Senate could ratify SALT II, however, things had begun to change again on the international scene. Throughout the 1960s and 1970s, the United States and the Soviet Union had moved away from the tensions of the cold war. The two sides had talked, negotiated, reached agreements. It was a period of cooperation, of détente. But as the 1980s began, the spirit of détente faded.

In December 1979, the Soviet Union invaded the nation of Afghanistan, on its southern border. That recalled the days of Soviet takeovers in Eastern Europe, and the United States reacted angrily. The cold war stirred into new life.

By January 1980, it seemed clear that the Senate was in no mood to ratify SALT II. That month President Carter withdrew the treaty from Senate consideration. The next year, a new United States president, Ronald Reagan, announced that SALT II was finished. He had no intention of asking for ratification.

An era of nuclear arms negotiations had come to an end. The emphasis had shifted from trying to control the arms race to escalating it by building more and more powerful and accurate new weapons. To many people around the world, that made all-out nuclear war seem more likely than ever before.

4. A Growing Arms Race

If nuclear war comes, it will be the Soviet Union that is responsible. That, in the early 1980s, was the view of most members of the United States government.

Just look at how the Soviets act, these government officials said. In 1979, they invaded Afghanistan. In 1981, they encouraged the Communist government of Poland to repress the working-class Solidarity union movement there. Through the years, they have suppressed freedom movements in other Eastern European countries. They have supported revolutions in such African nations as Angola and Ethiopia, in parts of Southeast Asia, and in South and Central America. Generally, these revolutions have been against governments friendly to the United States.

The Soviet Union says it wants peace, American officials say, but it prepares for war. Consider the recent Soviet nuclear arms buildup. In 1981, according to United States Department of Defense figures, the Soviet Union spent nearly $222 billion on its military. That same year, according to the department, the United States spent only $154 billion.

What have the Soviets been spending that money on? SS-20 missiles, for one thing. Today, hundreds of these intermediate-range ballistic missiles lie ready for action, targeted on Western Europe. The Soviets have also been spending money on multiwarheaded ICBMs. The result is a huge force of enormous land-based missiles that poses a serious threat to the smaller United States ICBM arsenal.

Not only have the Soviets succeeded in building more ICBMs than the United States, but the "throw-weight" of each of their missiles is also greater than ours. Throw-weight is the weight of the top stage of a missile. Total American throw-weight is just 4.2 million pounds. Soviet throw-weight is 11.2 million pounds.

The Soviet Union has spent money on technological improvements, too — on designing and building missiles that are increasingly accurate. Many United States military experts believe that the Soviet military buildup of the 1970s has given that country a "counter-force capability."

A counter-force capability is the ability to destroy so many of a country's ICBMs that that country would not be able to retaliate. In other words, the Soviets would strike against the United States once —

and the war would be over. America would have to surrender in abject defeat.

Until 1980, Americans did not hear much about Soviet counter-force capability. But in the presidential election campaign that year, Republican candidate Ronald Reagan made the phrase important. He charged that his opponent, Democratic President Jimmy Carter, had let the United States fall dangerously far behind the Soviet Union in the arms race. The United States had opened a "window of vulnerability" to the Soviets, he said.

Ronald Reagan won that election. When he became president, he made clear his plans for closing the "window of vulnerability." Those plans included going ahead with several new weapons systems.

One system was the MX missile. "MX" stands for missile experimental. Before he lost the 1980 election, President Carter had committed the country to building the MX, and Reagan was eager to carry out that commitment.

If it is built, the MX will provide the United States with a massive new ICBM force. Each missile will be 70 feet long and weigh 96 tons. Each will carry ten separate nuclear warheads. And each of those warheads will be thirty times more powerful than the Hiroshima bomb. Although the MX has never been fully tested, some experts think it could withstand a

Soviet first strike. After an attack, they say, enough MX missiles would survive to attack — and destroy — Soviet targets.

The neutron bomb is another new weapon that President Reagan favored building. This bomb is also known as an "enhanced radiation weapon." It is a hydrogen bomb that produces such an intense fusion reaction that it releases more energy as radiation than as blast.

Like any nuclear weapon, the neutron bomb would utterly destroy the area at the point of impact — ground zero. But in the area outside ground zero, damage to houses, factories, and other structures would be less than with ordinary nuclear weapons. Radiation effects, however, would be far greater. Over hundreds of acres, there would be no human survivors, and few other animals, or plants, would live. Within a hundred acres of ground zero, even insects, bacteria, algae, and fungi would be destroyed.

United States scientists and military experts have known since the 1950s that it was possible to build a neutron bomb, but they hesitated to do so. A weapon that is deliberately designed to do more damage to living things than to buildings and other objects is particularly immoral, many believed. But by 1981, United States plans definitely called for going ahead with the neutron bomb.

President Reagan also decided to develop a new SLBM, the Trident II. This missile will be more accurate and more deadly than the Trident I's now on United States submarines.

Finally, Reagan endorsed Carter's plan to deploy — base — 572 Pershing II and cruise missiles in Europe starting in late 1983. These highly sophisticated weapons are designed to counter the threat posed by Soviet SS-20s. Pershing II's, based in West Germany, would be able to reach their Soviet targets eight minutes after launch. They are designed to be powerful enough to destroy concrete-reinforced shelters as deep as 100 feet underground. Cruise missiles are slow and low-flying. Hugging the ground as they do, they cannot be detected by radar. They are quite accurate.

Weapons like the Pershing II and the MX are new kinds of weapons for the United States. They are intended to do more than simply to deter — to counter the threat of a Soviet first strike. They are, themselves, first-strike weapons. When — and if — these weapons are deployed, the United States might be able to launch such a devastating attack against the Soviet Union that the Soviets would not be able to strike back. Then America would be dictating peace terms to the Soviet Union, not the other way around.

Having terms dictated to them by the United States is exactly what Soviet leaders fear. From their point of view, it's Americans, not Soviets, who are most likely to be responsible for starting a nuclear war.

After all, the Soviets say, look how the United States acts. Through the years, the United States has backed dictatorships in Africa, Southeast Asia, and South and Central America that are trying to suppress revolutions in their countries. The Soviet Union supports such revolutionary movements. The United States also encourages movements hostile to the Soviets in Poland and the other nations of Eastern Europe. It acted outraged when the Soviet Union went into Afghanistan — but that action was none of America's business.

The United States says it wants peace, Soviet officials say, but it prepares for war. Consider the recent American nuclear arms buildup. America claims it spends less on its military than the Soviet Union does, but together with the other NATO countries, the United States outspends the Communist Warsaw Pact nations. The Soviets add that United States Department of Defense figures may not be reliable. According to the Stockholm International Peace Research Institute (SIPRI), in Sweden, the Soviet Union spends slightly *less* than the United States. Other figures echo the SIPRI estimates. In March 1983, the U.S. Central Intelligence Agency (CIA) reported its conclusion that Americans have been overestimating recent Soviet military expenditures. Each country spent about $154 billion in 1981, CIA officials said.

What has the United States been spending its money on? No sooner was SALT I signed in 1972, the Soviet leaders say, than the United States began a massive MIRV program. Soon, the United States had so many MIRVed missiles that the Soviet Union was compelled to begin a MIRV program of its own.

As for American fears about the throw-weight of Soviet missiles, that is beside the point. The high Soviet throw-weight is only an indication that American missiles are technically superior to those of the Soviet Union. Throw-weight includes everything that one country "delivers" to another — the missile nose cone, re-entry vehicle, computer guidance system, and mechanical gear, as well as the actual warhead. Throw-weight has little to do with a missile's effectiveness. For example, when the United States replaced the warheads on its Minuteman missiles, each Minuteman's throw-weight went up by 35 pounds, from 2000 pounds to 2035. But the improvements increased the explosive force of each warhead from 170 kilotons of TNT (170,000 tons) to 335 kilotons.

Soviet leaders also maintain that American missiles have improved in accuracy even more than their own have. In fact, many American experts believe that the Soviets are convinced that no matter how hard they try, they will never quite catch up with American technology. They say this is a big reason the Soviets are so determined to forge ahead with new weapons systems.

Officials in Moscow also remind us that even if they wiped out every single one of America's land-based ICBMs, they would have destroyed only one-quarter of this country's nuclear arsenal. Only 25 percent of U.S. nuclear weapons are ICBMs. Another 25 percent are bombs that would be dropped from long-range bombers. In 1982, the United States had 348 bombers, compared to 140 for the Soviet Union.

Furthermore, a full 50 percent of America's nuclear force consists of SLBMs. SLBMs, like weapons in bombers, can easily be moved around and hidden from enemy attack. So even if the United States lost all its ICBMs, it would still have 75 percent of its nuclear weapons left with which to launch counter-attacks from submarines. By contrast, a United States attack that disabled all Soviet ICBMs would destroy about 71 percent of Soviet nuclear weapons.

Given such facts, Soviet leaders say, American talk about a window of vulnerability is nonsense. The window is no more real than the bomber gap was, or the missile gap. Many Americans believed in those gaps in the 1950s and 1960s, but neither one existed. Soviet leaders think it's the same today. The so-called window does not really exist.

Even the United States Department of Defense seems to share the Soviet view on this. In its 1981 annual report, the department said: "While the era of United States superiority is long past, parity — not United States inferiority — has replaced it."

But even if the two nations are at parity, some U.S. officials believe, that isn't good enough. The United States must not rest until it is once again far ahead of the Soviet Union. One of President Reagan's 1980 campaign promises was to regain U.S. "nuclear superiority." To win that superiority, the Reagan administration asked Congress to agree to spend $1.5 trillion on the military over a five-year period. Later, that figure was raised to $1.6 trillion, and still later, to $1.8 trillion. (That is a very large figure. It is estimated that, over an average human lifespan of about 75 years, a person's heart will beat three billion times. So if someone gave you $600 dollars for every one of your heartbeats, it would still take you three-quarters of a century to earn $1.8 trillion.)

From the point of view of Soviet leaders, it's a scary picture. The United States will not give up the arms race until it has an overwhelming first-strike capability. It will not be satisfied until the Soviet Union is clearly a second-rate nuclear power.

From the point of view of United States leaders, it's a scary picture. The Soviet Union will not give up the arms race until it has an overwhelming first-strike capability. It will not be satisfied until the United States is clearly a second-rate nuclear power.

From the point of view of the rest of us — the 4.5 billion men, women, and children who share this earth — it's a scary picture. The arms race is rocketing out of control. And history teaches us that an arms race generally leads to war. "It is sobering to remember," wrote one American statesman, "that modern history offers no example of the cultivation by rival powers of armed force on a massive scale which did not in the end lead to an outbreak of hostilities."

How might nuclear hostilities start? One answer is: by accident.

In June 1980, military personnel at United States Air Force Strategic Air Command (SAC) in Omaha, Nebraska, were routinely monitoring a missile warning system. Suddenly the computer indicated that large numbers of Soviet SLBMs were heading for the United States mainland! The SAC commander acted quickly. He ordered the crews of more than a hundred B-52 bombers to ready their aircraft for takeoff. Each B-52 carries four nuclear warheads.

Fortunately for all of us, the B-52s never left the ground. A check with a Colorado base revealed that no missiles were on the way. The Omaha computer had simply malfunctioned. A few days later, another, similar alert occurred. This time, the computer showed an attack by Soviet ICBMs.

Many such false alarms have taken place. In one eighteen-month period, there were 151 of them. Once, United States forces were on nuclear alert for more than six minutes.

In the future, the problem of malfunctioning computers may be even worse. New weapons systems on both sides will rely more and more upon computers to launch attacks. "Neither the Soviet Union nor the United States has any intention of launching a nuclear attack," says Arthur Macy Cox, an American arms-control expert, "but if both sides deploy the next round of nuclear weapons, the risk of war by accident will increase from possible to probable."

In the past, when a computer went haywire, human beings could step in, run a check, and correct the error. Soon, that may not be possible. Computers will gather information — and act on it — even if that information is wrong.

Being wrong wouldn't bother a computer. People want to avoid war. They will check and double-check the information they receive. Computers won't. Computers couldn't care less if the whole world disappears in radioactive smoke and ashes.

Nuclear war could start in other ways. A small band of terrorists could build a nuclear weapon and use it against a target. Forty years ago, the secrets of nuclear physics were known to only a few brilliant scientists. Today it is possible for a college student with a flair for physics to construct a small nuclear device. Except for uranium and plutonium, the materials are not hard to find. And uranium and plutonium have been known to disappear from government labs and private plants. In 1976, government officials reported "tens of tons" of weapons materials, including uranium and plutonium, were missing from nuclear facilities in the United States. Who has those materials now? No one knows.

Nuclear weapons materials may be even more available to terrorists in Europe. The U.S. Central Intelligence Agency says that American missile installations there are unsafe and vulnerable. They foresee a "moderate likelihood" of terrorist attack at several bases. After a tour of NATO bases in Europe, one United States senator called security there "terrible."

By itself, a small group of terrorists could not start an all-out nuclear war. But suppose one of the superpowers had reason to believe that the terrorists were acting at the orders of the other superpower? Suppose a nuclear weapon went off without warning in New York or Chicago? Would United States officials take the time to investigate slowly and carefully? Or would they assume the country was under Soviet attack and react accordingly?

It wouldn't even take a terrorist to start a nuclear war. If an American or Soviet military commander suddenly went berserk and started falsifying computer information or issuing insane orders, war could result. Over 100,000 men and women in the American military work with nuclear weaponry. In 1977, according to one congressional committee, 256 of them were dismissed from their jobs because they were alcoholics. Five times that number were fired for taking drugs. And 1219 more were laid off because they were found to have mental disorders. Without question, there are disturbed people and alcoholics among the men and women in charge of Soviet nuclear weapons, too.

Nuclear war could also result from the American and Soviet habit of playing politics on a worldwide scale. Each superpower has allies around the globe. Most of these allies are engaged in their own rivalries and conflicts, rivalries and conflicts that reflect those of the superpowers. For instance, in the Middle East, the United States is allied to Israel, the Soviet Union to the Arab nations with which Israel has repeatedly gone to war.

Suppose a new war breaks out between Israel and an Arab state. Neither the United States nor the Soviet Union would want to see its ally defeated. When defeat for one side does seem possible, that side's superpower ally might begin supplying it with tactical nuclear weapons. A "small" nuclear war would have begun.

It could grow. The other superpower might respond by giving nuclear arms to its ally. Then the first superpower would make more, and more powerful, weapons available. Eventually, one superpower might decide to "punish" the other for supplying weapons in the first place. It would launch a major nuclear strike against the other superpower's homeland. Or perhaps the other superpower, fearing just such a pre-emptive first strike, would launch an ICBM attack of its own. A full-scale nuclear war would be under way. Many experts believe such a scenario for nuclear war is the most likely.

However, the Soviet Union and the United States are not the only nations that could start a nuclear war. Britain, France, China, and India are also nuclear powers. Any one of them could use nuclear weapons in some part of the world. From there, the war could spread to involve Americans and Soviets.

In 1982, for instance, Britain fought a ten-week war against Argentina in the South Atlantic Ocean. According to reports, Britain sent tactical nuclear weapons to the scene. These weapons were not used. What if they had been? The United States backed

Britain in the war; the Soviet Union sided with Argentina. If British nuclear weapons had killed Argentine soldiers and sailors, or damaged their ships and planes, would the Soviet Union have stood idly by?

The spread of nuclear weapons to countries throughout the world is another problem that is bound to grow. Today, there are six nuclear nations. By the year 2000, a total of thirty-one countries may possess nuclear arms. So said a 1982 United States intelligence survey.

The thirty-one nations include several, such as Pakistan, Iran, Iraq, and Israel, that have unfriendly relations with neighboring countries. Wars are frequent among some of these nations. Other countries that may soon have nuclear capability are governed by harsh, unpopular regimes: South Africa, South Korea, Taiwan, Argentina, and the Philippines are examples. Many people fear the leaders of such countries might find it hard to resist using nuclear weapons, even against their own people, if they had them.

The Nuclear Non-Proliferation Treaty, adopted by the United States and the Soviet Union in 1968, was supposed to stop the spread of nuclear weapons. But forty-five countries have not even signed the treaty.

What's more, despite the treaty, the Soviet Union and the United States continue to supply the world with nuclear materials and technology. Each super-

power insists that it has the right to help friendly
nations develop nuclear energy for peaceful purposes — for medicine and industry, and to generate
electricity. But "peaceful" nuclear plants can easily
be converted into bomb factories.

Some years ago, Canada sold a nuclear reactor to
India. Before agreeing to the sale, Canadian officials
got India to promise to use the reactor only for non-
military purposes. But the Indian government did not
keep its word. In 1974, using materials produced by
the reactor, India exploded its first nuclear weapon.

Oddly enough, that did not slow down the sale of
nuclear materials to nonnuclear nations. President
Carter agreed to sell 38 tons of enriched uranium to
India *after* that country tested its bomb. In 1982, the
Reagan administration began easing the rules for
providing nuclear fuel and technology to other nations. This country has started making uranium and
plutonium more readily available to countries including Brazil, Argentina, and South Africa. It has
promised to help France build its own neutron bomb.

Will one of these countries one day start a small
nuclear war that somehow engulfs more and more
countries — and turns into a big nuclear war?

Or will it be one of the superpowers that — quite
deliberately and cold-bloodedly — starts a nuclear
war?

Both the United States and the Soviet Union have detailed plans for fighting a nuclear war. We don't know much about the Soviets' plans. They have a closed, secretive, society. Only a few top officials know what is going on in the government. Outsiders only hear about the plans and programs that Soviet leaders want them to hear about.

But we can make guesses. We know Soviet leaders are spending billions of dollars on the arms race. And we know that this is money the country cannot really afford to spend on weapons.

The ordinary people of the Soviet Union lack many of the consumer goods that we take for granted. They have fewer clothes than most of us, and poorer food. Few people own cars. Housing is in short supply. Television sets, stereos, expensive sports equipment, which are practically necessities to us, are luxuries in the Soviet Union. If Soviet leaders switched their spending from armaments to consumer goods, the nation's standard of living might improve.

The government is unwilling to make that switch, though. That is one indication that the Soviet Union is serious about preparing for war.

Another indication comes from some of the few Soviet reports and articles that do find their way to the outside world. According to one article, Soviet military leaders are not only planning for a nuclear war, they are planning to win one. "There is profound error and harm," wrote a leading Soviet general, "in the disorienting claims that there will be no victor in a thermonuclear world war." Those are ominous words. A great many scientists and other experts in both the United States and the Soviet Union believe that all-out nuclear war would destroy civilization. That belief is an important part of what makes deterrence work.

Yet another indication that the Soviets are preparing for nuclear war lies in their civil defense planning. Soviet leaders are making elaborate plans to protect themselves and their government in the event of nuclear war. They are trying to devise ways to guard their factories and factory workers. In addition, they have plans for mass evacuations — for getting city dwellers out of their homes and into the countryside as soon as they have warning that an American attack is coming. According to CIA reports, Soviet plans call for people to evacuate on foot, carrying their belongings. That's because so few Soviet citizens have cars. There is little public transportation outside the cities.

The United States government is also making war plans and setting up civil defense programs. We know more about them than we do about Soviet plans. The United States is an open society, a democracy. Many men and women, at all levels of government, know what is going on. So does the public.

One thing we know is that some United States officials believe it would be possible to fight a nuclear war — and win it. In 1982, the U.S. Department of Defense issued a 125-page report that accepts the idea that we could defeat the Soviet Union in a nuclear war that lasts for weeks or even months. In such a war, the report said, American nuclear forces "must prevail and be able to force the Soviet Union to seek earliest termination of hostilities on terms favorable to the United States."

Does that mean the Department of Defense considers nuclear war "winnable"? news reporters asked the secretary of defense, Caspar Weinberger, in 1982. Weinberger said it did not. But, he added, "we are certainly not planning to be defeated." Puzzled reporters wondered what Weinberger was planning on, if he had ruled out both victory and defeat.

Actually, the answer is simple. The Defense Department does have a strategy for winning a nuclear war. This strategy is known as "decapitation."

To decapitate means to cut off the head. One American plan calls for cutting off Soviet leaders from their people in a nuclear war. Swift missile attacks would kill all the nation's political and military leaders and destroy its lines of communication. The Soviet people would have no choice but to surrender. (How they would negotiate terms of a surrender without leadership and with no communication throughout their vast nation, the report does not explain.)

Along with planning for attacks on the Soviet Union, American officials are preparing ways to meet the threat of Soviet attacks on this country. FEMA — the Federal Emergency Management Agency — has 3000 employees around the nation. They are busy designing evacuation programs for every town and city with 50,000 or more inhabitants. They are also arranging for evacuations of towns near 400 different military installations. The scheme for evacuating the residents of Burlington, Beacon Falls, and Bethlehem, Connecticut, to Becket, Massachusetts, is a FEMA plan.

In March 1982, President Reagan asked Congress to spend $4.3 billion on nuclear civil defense by 1990. With that kind of money, he said, 80 percent of all Americans would survive a nuclear war.

Under FEMA's plans, people would move in an orderly way from cities and other target areas into the country. (Before you go, FEMA suggests that you lock the dog and cat in the cellar with a two-week supply of food and water.) Buses and trains will carry those who do not have cars. People who do have cars will get to go first, however; others will have to wait. What if your car breaks down or runs out of gas? Don't worry. "Prepositioned bulldozers" will push you off the road.

Where will you get food and other supplies while you're away from your "home area"? FEMA expects private companies to supply it. Mail will be delivered, naturally. The United States Postal Service already has change-of-address cards prepared for nuclear refugees to fill out as they flee. There will also be taxes to pay. Since government officials expect that all income tax records will be destroyed in a nuclear war, they plan to place a flat 20 percent tax on all goods sold.

How will you protect yourself from radioactivity? "Dig a hole," a deputy undersecretary of defense, Thomas K. Jones, recommended. "Cover it with a couple of doors and then throw three feet of dirt on top. It's the dirt that does it." Jones was optimistic about your chances of surviving. "Everybody's going to make it if there are enough shovels to go around," he reassured the nation.

Within two or three weeks, the war will be over and you'll go home. Be sure to take some food along. As FEMA points out: "Fuel and food supplies will be rerouted to your home area; however, this may take a day or two . . . It may be necessary to take extra precaution with waste. Some food stocks will probably have to be carried back in your car. Be sure it is fresh, particularly raw meat."

Is this kind of civil defense planning realistic? Remember government predictions of what would happen if a single one-megaton bomb were dropped on Detroit. Would anyone at all, much less 80 percent of us, survive an all-out nuclear war? Many Americans think the answer is "Of course not." Like the antinuclear activists who formed BOMBS and BLAST, they believe such plans are not really intended to be put into operation. They think civil defense planning is designed to reassure Americans about nuclear war, and to persuade them that they probably would live through one. At the same time, the elaborate plans are supposed to scare the Soviets, and convince them that the United States would not hesitate to risk nuclear war under some circumstances. If the people who think this way are correct, most nuclear civil defense planning is a giant bluff.

But most people are convinced that some emergency planning is perfectly serious. They believe that plans for protecting top government officials are carefully thought out, and that they are ready to be put into effect instantly if the occasion arises.

If nuclear war comes, the president will be flown by helicopter to a specially designed jet. Surrounded by leather swivel chairs, soft carpeting, color-coordinated telephones, and sophisticated office equipment, he will issue orders from far above the scene of mass destruction.

In an article in the *New York Times,* Stephen F. Cohen, professor of politics at Princeton University, pointed out that while ordinary citizens are battling traffic jams and fear-maddened crowds to save themselves and their families, government officials and *their* families will be tucked safely away in "hollowed mountains, special aircraft, and superhardened bunkers." Cohen continued, "No wonder leaders can authorize plans for the instant incineration and radiation of millions of people; they expect to be elsewhere."

Millions of Americans share Cohen's cynical view. So do millions of Soviets.

Many Soviet citizens, like many Americans, believe that civil defense planning for leaders is a reality — but for ordinary people, a sham. Can you imagine walking away from a nuclear war? Like so many in this country, people in the Soviet Union joke bitterly about emergency planning. They call their civil defense plan "grob," which is a shortened form of the program's full Russian name — Grazhdanskaya Oborona. But "grob" also means "coffin" in Russian.

A coffin is just about all the average Soviet can expect if nuclear war comes. Actually, of course, he or she wouldn't get even that — or a funeral or a formal burial, either. Just death. Death is about all the average American in a targeted area can expect, too.

It wouldn't matter who started the war, the United States or the Soviet Union. It wouldn't matter if India and Pakistan started it, or Brazil, or a fanatical group of terrorists. It wouldn't matter if it started by accident or as a result of superpower politics in the Middle East or elsewhere. The results would be the same.

Millions of people around the world recognize that fact. That is why they are marching and demonstrating and speaking out against nuclear war and the nuclear arms race.

5. Antinuclear Activity

Brice Lalonde and his crew of four brought their 38-foot sailboat, *Greenpeace III,* to within a few miles of land and dropped anchor. Tensely, they scanned sky and sea for signs of trouble.

Behind them, somewhere out in the vast South Pacific Ocean, two mine sweepers of the French Navy were searching for their small boat. The French captains had urgent orders to intercept the *Greenpeace,* board her, and, at all costs, prevent her crew members from carrying out their mission.

Before the *Greenpeace* lay the little island of Moruroa. Moruroa, with its graceful volcanic mountains, lush, colorful flowers, and waving palm trees, has been called a tropical paradise.

It has also been called a piece of radioactive Swiss cheese, and it is that description that had brought Lalonde and his crew there.

Moruroa is part of French Polynesia. Beginning in the early 1960s, France used the island as a testing ground for nuclear weapons. Before 1975, many of these tests took place in the atmosphere. Since then, nearly a hundred nuclear devices have been detonated underground. The blasts have badly damaged Moruroa's brittle coral and basalt foundation, and scientists say the island has sunk five feet in the last twenty years. Cracks, some as wide as eighteen inches and as long as half a mile, have appeared on the island. Piles of radioactive waste dot its beaches. Often, contaminated tools and equipment are washed out to sea.

The destruction of Moruroa and the poisoning of the sea and air around it worry Brice Lalonde. Lalonde is the leader of a small French political party called L'Ecologie (Ecology). In 1981, he decided to protest his nation's nuclear weapons testing on Moruroa.

Lalonde's plan was to make it as difficult as possible for French military authorities to carry out the tests scheduled for the fall of 1981. Aboard the *Greenpeace,* he and his crew kept just outside Moruroa's twelve-mile territorial limit — and just inside the island's "danger zone." No one is allowed within this danger zone while testing is going on.

For days, the *Greenpeace* played hide-and-seek with the two mine sweepers. But in the end, the navy's superior size and speed won out. *Greenpeace III* was overtaken and forced to retreat.

Yet Lalonde was not dissatisfied. He had focused

world attention on French nuclear testing. Furthermore, the French government agreed to let him take part in a scientific investigation of the ways nuclear testing may be affecting the environment of the South Pacific and the health of its people.

Lalonde's antinuclear protest is not the only one that has taken place in the South Pacific. A few thousand miles northwest of Moruroa lie the Marshall Islands. These islands have been owned and administered by the United States since World War II. Among them is the Kwajalein Atoll, a United States nuclear test site. Missile delivery systems (not actual warheads), fired from Vandenberg Air Force Base in California, land regularly on Kwajalein. In the future, the U.S. government plans to use the atoll to test a new antiballistic missile system.

Many Marshall Islanders are unhappy at this prospect. Early in 1982, eight hundred of them began camping out near the Kwajalein test range. For four months, they refused to leave. Finally they did go home, but not until the United States agreed to cut twenty years from its fifty-year agreement to test on Kwajalein.

Whittling twenty years from a fifty-year testing agreement may not sound like much of a victory. By itself, it will do little to limit United States nuclear arms development. Nor will Lalonde's protest keep his government from continuing its nuclear tests in

French Polynesia. Even so, antinuclear activists are encouraged by the protests in the South Pacific. Every action that is taken anywhere on earth against nuclear weapons and the nuclear arms race, they believe, is an important step in the worldwide effort to avoid the devastation of nuclear war.

The possibility of such a war is very much on the minds of many Europeans. They feel they have special reason to fear it. Unless the arms race stops, they think, their homelands will become a nuclear battleground for the Soviet Union and the United States.

Why do Europeans worry? Since World War II ended, the two superpowers have stood ready to fight each other in Europe. NATO and Warsaw Pact troops, each armed with nuclear and conventional weapons, glare at each other across the continent.

Thirty years ago, Western Europe had a strong antinuclear movement. But as time went by, interest in nuclear problems there faded. After the United States and the Soviet Union began serious arms-control negotiations, Europeans tried to ignore the possibility of war. Deterrence seemed to be working, the European military balance holding. On the Warsaw Pact side was a moderate nuclear force and a large conventional one. On the NATO side was the reverse — a large nuclear force and a moderate conventional one.

Then, in 1977, the Soviets began deploying intermediate-range SS-20s to counter the threat of NATO's nuclear force. Worried by this, West European leaders appealed to President Carter to base new U.S. intermediate-range weapons — the Pershing II and cruise missiles — in their nations. President Carter considered the request for two years before he agreed to it. In 1979, he announced that Pershing II's would be based in West Germany, and cruise missiles in West Germany, Italy, the Netherlands, Belgium, and Britain. Basing, which would take about five years, would begin in late 1983. Only if the Soviet Union dismantled their SS-20s before then, the president said, would the United States drop its deployment plans. The arms race was heating up.

So was talk of war — of war in Europe. Soviet leaders spoke of it. So, after he became president, did Ronald Reagan. "You could have an exchange of tactical weapons against troops in the field," he told reporters — and he meant the field in Europe — "without it bringing either one of the major powers to pushing the button." In other words, the United States could fight it out with the Soviet Union in Europe without endangering its own lands and people.

Other American and Soviet leaders have made it clear they would not hesitate to be the first to use nuclear weapons in Europe in certain cases. NATO commanders have always said they would use nuclear weapons if necessary to beat back any strong

Soviet attack with conventional weapons. For their part, the Soviets hinted that they might well launch a pre-emptive strike against any Pershing II's based in West Germany.

The Soviets also warned that deployment of the Pershing II's, which could reach their targets in just eight minutes, might cause them to go to a "launch on warning" strategy. Launch on warning means that Soviet missiles would automatically be fired the instant computerized early warning networks indicated an attack. That firing would be "ordered" by computer, not by a human being. Experts believe launch on warning would greatly increase the chance of accidental war. Furthermore, if one superpower goes to launch on warning, it is almost certain that the other will quickly do the same.

Such facts and statements, and the decision by both sides to deploy their newest weapons, helped reawaken the European antinuclear movement. "Nuclear weapons had gone to the back of our minds," explained one European activist, a Norwegian mathematician. "But we were becoming more aware of the arms buildup, and suddenly realized that they were planning to *use* those nuclear weapons. We felt angry and cheated."

Anger led to action. In 1980, a group of West Germans — religious leaders, environmentalists, and members of youth organizations — met in the town of Krefeld on the Rhine River. There, they drew up the Krefeld Manifesto. It called on the West German government to withdraw its request for the deployment of the new U.S. missiles. Within weeks, the manifesto had two hundred thousand signatures; a year later, more than a million and a half.

A new European antinuclear movement was growing. Soon, it included a wide range of people — students, scientists, laborers, doctors, lawyers, housewives, and teachers — and lots of them. In 1981, one public-opinion poll showed that 53 percent of Britons wanted to see all United States military bases in their country closed down. In West Germany, 39 percent opposed the new missile deployment and only 29 percent supported it. In the Netherlands, 68 percent were against deployment. Most of those who opposed deployment said they were convinced that if the United States agreed to drop its plans for new missiles, the Soviet Union would reciprocate by dismantling its SS-20s.

To let their leaders know how they felt, European protesters took to the streets. Two hundred fifty thousand rallied in Bonn, the capital of West Germany, on October 10, 1981. Two weeks later, 175,000 marched through London and 200,000 through Rome. Other demonstrations took place in Belgium, France, and Norway. The next month, 400,000 gathered in Madrid, Spain.

Can such demonstrations have an effect on the leaders of Western Europe? In West Germany, fifty-eight members of the Bundestag (national legislature) announced their support of the Bonn march. The man who was the main speaker at the rally in Madrid, Felipe González, was elected president of Spain a year later. British demonstrators listened to an antinuclear pep talk by the head of the Labour party, one of the country's major political parties. But in 1981, these leaders were exceptions. Most Western European government officials agreed that the new U.S. missiles were needed to ensure continued nuclear deterrence.

Yet for many European activists, trying to stop the 1983 deployment seemed to be just the first step in a larger antinuclear movement. Their aim is to get all nuclear weapons — American, Soviet, British, and French — off European soil. Only complete multilateral nuclear disarmament, they believe, will keep Europe from being turned into radioactive ruins and ashes.

"Arms control, the step-by-step approach, has not worked," according to Mient Jan Faber, an antinuclear activist from the Netherlands. "Our overall goal — all nuclear weapons out of Europe — will be a long process," he told followers, "but it can begin here."

Moving away from a step-by-step approach could

even mean unilateral disarmament — disarmament by the NATO countries alone. This prospect does not faze some European activists. They are convinced that if NATO makes a unilateral decision to begin disarming, the Soviet Union will follow suit. Unilateral disarmament will turn into bilateral disarmament. Europe will be freed of its burden of nuclear weapons.

Other Europeans are still more radical. They seek unilateral NATO nuclear disarmament — regardless of what the Soviets do. If that means NATO ends up with no nuclear weapons at all, while the Pact countries remain heavily armed with both nuclear and conventional weapons, then so be it. And if that leads to the Soviet Union taking over the nations of Western Europe, that's all right, too, the most radical unilateralists say. They believe that nuclear war must be avoided, no matter what the cost.

Calls for disarmament can be heard even from Communist Eastern Europe. In East Germany, the antinuclear movement began with members of the clergy, especially with ministers of the Lutheran Church. Most of those who joined the movement were young. They adopted a peace symbol — a sword beaten into a ploughshare — which they displayed on badges and armbands.

Occasionally, protests have occurred within the Soviet Union. In July 1982, three hundred women from the Scandinavian nations of Norway, Sweden, and Denmark got permission from the Soviet government to hold antinuclear rallies in three Russian cities. A small Soviet antinuclear group even made its appearance in 1982. When it was formed, the group had just eleven members.

The new antinuclear movement started small in the United States, too. It began in 1979, with the idea of "freezing" the arms race. The freeze proposal was the brain child of the American Friends Service Committee, a Quaker group, and a woman named Randall Forsberg.

Randall Forsberg's interest in nuclear weapons began when she was a typist at the Stockholm International Peace Research Institute. After she left her job in Sweden and returned home to the United States, she studied military policy and arms control at the Massachusetts Institute of Technology. Today, she heads a group of arms-control experts at the Institute for Defense and Disarmament Studies.

Forsberg describes the freeze as "a mere, slight first step" toward a world in which instant annihilation is not a constant threat. The proposal has two parts. "The first is stopping the production of nuclear warheads," she says. "The second . . . is to stop the steady advances in technology, in the delivery systems associated with nuclear weapons."

Forsberg believes that if the Soviet Union and the

United States agree to adopt a freeze, it will give the two nations a sort of breathing space. They can use that breathing space to discuss ways to reduce the number of nuclear weapons each side owns. That is what makes the freeze idea different from earlier arms-control proposals. As we have seen, the United States and the Soviet Union have signed weapons treaties in the past, yet the total number of weapons in the world continues to go up, not down.

This freeze proposal is not the first one ever made. The Soviet Union suggested freezes in every year from 1976 to 1980. The United States government refused to consider them.

Other freeze proposals were American. In 1964, President Lyndon Johnson offered to halt American nuclear weapons production if the Soviet Union would do the same. The Soviet Union would not. Six years later, the United States Senate voted in favor of a freeze resolution, but nothing came of it.

The backers of the new freeze proposals were determined that this time things would be different. As a first step, they decided to try to work through the nation's political system. In 1980, they asked the leaders of the Democratic party to adopt the freeze proposal and work to get a freeze resolution through Congress.

Democratic leaders turned the idea down flat. It "terrified" most of them, according to one party leader who did support the freeze. Top Democrats, he added, feared that if they supported the proposal, members of the Republican party would accuse them of being "soft" on the Soviet Union.

Not all Americans were equally terrified. Some were beginning to speak out against the arms race.

For example, there was Roger Molander, an arms-control expert at the United States Department of Defense and a member of the National Security Council staff during the 1970s. One day at a staff meeting, Molander listened as a navy captain claimed that people are unnecessarily upset about the idea of nuclear war. As he remembered it later, "the captain added that people were talking as if nuclear war would be the end of the world, when in fact, only 500 million would be killed."

Molander thought about that for a while. "Only 500 million! Only 500 million! Only one-eighth of the world's population!" Before long he had resigned his job and founded an antinuclear group called Ground Zero.

Another newly formed organization was the Center for Defense Information (CDI). It specializes in gathering and analyzing Defense Department reports and other military information. Although this group believes that the United States needs a strong military, it argues that the nuclear arms buildup of the Reagan administration is both unnecessary and dangerous. The group's director and deputy director are retired rear admirals of the United States Navy. One of its three associate directors is a former major general in the Army. The other two were Marine Corps officers. The actor Paul Newman is a board member.

The Center for Defense Information and Ground Zero were not the only new antinuclear groups. In the early 1980s, men, women, and children were organizing in every part of the country. There were Dancers for Disarmament, Nurses for a Nonnuclear Future, the Children's Peace Committee, Social Workers for Nuclear Disarmament, Physicians for Social Responsibility, Women Against Military Madness, and many more. In Minnesota, a group of sports fishermen began calling themselves Anglers for Nuclear Disarmament. Older, established antinuclear groups included the Union of Concerned Scientists, the American Federation of Scientists, and the Committee for a Sane Nuclear Policy, SANE, for short.

Members of such groups met to talk about nuclear issues. Scientists, including some who worked on the Manhattan Project, spoke against continuing the arms race. Priests, ministers, and rabbis made nuclear war the subject of sermons. Teachers offered courses on nuclear war — how it might come about, what its effects might be, how it might be avoided. People discussed nuclear matters with their families, friends, and co-workers, trying to convince them that a nuclear freeze could succeed in slowing down, or even stopping, the arms race.

The idea spread quickly. During the spring of 1982, people at more than 250 town meetings in New England passed nuclear freeze resolutions. These resolutions required town officials to ask the president of the United States to offer a formal freeze proposal to the Soviet Union. Public-opinion polls showed that a huge majority of Americans — 87 percent of them — supported a nuclear freeze that would leave the United States and the Soviet Union at parity. Around the country, hundreds of thousands of antinuclear activists participated in mass rallies and demonstrations.

Where people lead the way, politicians may follow. City council members in various parts of the country began endorsing freeze resolutions. At their 1982 convention, the mayors of 500 American cities voted in favor of a freeze. So, at their own 1982 convention, did leaders of the Democratic party.

Now Democrats rushed to sponsor freeze resolutions in Congress. So did some Republicans. One resolution was introduced jointly by Senator Edward Kennedy of Massachusetts, a Democrat, and Senator Mark Hatfield of Oregon, a Republican. Both men had been concerned about nuclear weapons for years, but neither had sponsored a freeze until it became clear that the public wanted one. "The people are ahead of the politicians," Senator Hatfield commented wryly.

The senators worded their resolution carefully. It called for the Soviet Union and the United States to negotiate a "mutual and verifiable" freeze on nuclear weapons. "Mutual" meant that the two sides would make equal commitments. "Verifiable" meant that each side could make sure the other side was not cheating.

What would be negotiated under the freeze? Suggestions included a comprehensive test ban, a halt to production of strategic missiles and delivery systems, and control over tactical weapons. The freeze would probably last five years. During that time, the two sides would talk about future arms reductions.

While members of Congress were considering nuclear matters in political terms, others were looking at them from a moral point of view. The nation's Roman Catholic bishops, for instance, were reconsidering their Church's position on the arms race. Until the 1980s, most of the Catholic leadership had regarded an American nuclear buildup as necessary in order to defend this country against the Soviet Union. Now, many Church leaders were having second thoughts.

At their national conference in Washington, D.C.,

in November 1982, the country's three hundred bishops debated the morality of nuclear weapons. Although a few of the bishops spoke in favor of enlarging United States stockpiles, most opposed doing so. "We are stewards of a world God created," proclaimed Bishop Leroy Matthiesen of Amarillo, Texas, "and our task is to keep it good. We have messed it up in the past and now we are at a point where we can mess it up forever; we can literally undo creation."

Before the conference ended, the bishops voted overwhelmingly in favor of a pastoral letter that denounced nuclear weapons and labeled them as immoral according to the teachings of Christianity.

The letter also questioned the morality of the theory of deterrence. The bishops pointed out that deterrence promises to destroy millions of innocent civilians in a retaliatory second strike — a second strike that may not come until after the retaliating country has already lost the war. Such deterrence boils down to simple revenge. "No Christian can rightfully carry out orders or policies deliberately aimed at killing noncombatants," the letter said. Only if deterrence is combined with serious negotiations for arms reductions, the bishops concluded, can it be considered acceptable.

In adopting their pastoral letter, the bishops acted

independently of the head of the Church, Pope John Paul II. However, most felt that the Pope was signaling his approval when, a few weeks later, he promoted one of the most outspoken antinuclear bishops to cardinal.

Other Americans were trying to come up with other suggestions for ways to halt the nuclear arms race and to avert nuclear war. One idea came from four former government officials. The four were McGeorge Bundy, national security adviser from 1961 to 1966; George Kennan, former ambassador to the Soviet Union; Robert McNamara, secretary of defense from 1961 to 1968; and Gerard Smith, who led the SALT I negotiations. Their proposal appeared in a 1982 issue of *Foreign Affairs* magazine. It called for the United States and NATO to adopt a "no-first-use" nuclear policy in Europe.

A policy of no first use would require NATO leaders to pledge never to be the first to use nuclear weapons in Europe. It would be a direct reversal of the first-use strategy that NATO has followed from its beginning.

The four men made it clear why they were suggesting such a policy. "We have come to believe in a policy of no first use as imperative for the long-run survival of our society, and indeed of civilization as we know it," they wrote.

Those words made sense to millions in America and Europe. But in both places, there were some who believed that adopting a no-first-use policy — like offering a nuclear freeze or like failing to deploy new IRBMs in Europe — threatened disaster.

6.   Antinuclear—and Un-American?

From the start, some people were convinced that the antinuclear movement endangered American national security and world peace. They were sure that the movement, here and in Europe, was organized by the leaders of the Soviet Union and directed from the Kremlin, the Soviet seat of government.

President Reagan repeated that charge several times. The antinuclear movement, he told an Ohio audience in October 1982, was "inspired by not the sincere, honest people who want peace, but by some who want the weakening of America." Those who wanted the weakening of America, in the president's opinion, included Communists, Socialists, and members of other left-wing political groups.

Reporters questioned the president about his views at a news conference the next month. Reagan maintained that there was "plenty of evidence" to back him up. "There is no question about foreign agents that were sent to help instigate and help create and keep such a movement going," he added. Senator

Jeremiah Denton of Alabama thought the president was right. Members of antinuclear groups give "aid and comfort to the enemies of this country," he said.

In December, the president repeated his accusations. "Well-intentioned though it might be," he told reporters, "this movement might be carrying water that they're not aware of for another purpose." *Carrying water for another purpose* was the president's way of saying *acting in ways that help the Soviet Union.* "Incidentally," he went on, not very grammatically, "the first man who proposed the nuclear freeze was in February 21, 1981, in Moscow, Leonid Brezhnev."

How true are such charges? As far as who first proposed a freeze is concerned, the president was wrong. The freeze proposal under discussion in the 1980s was written in 1979 by Randall Forsberg and others. Several, slightly different, versions of it exist. Before that, freezes were suggested by the Soviet Union at least as early as 1976, and by President Johnson as far back as 1964.

The president made another mistake when he lumped the United States and European antinuclear movements together. There are great differences between them.

In Europe, the movement began because of people's worry about the planned deployment of new sophisticated missiles there. Its primary aim was to prevent new generations of United States weapons from being based in Europe. To that, some added another goal: that of eventually ridding the continent of all nuclear weapons — complete multilateral nuclear disarmament. A few, more radical, activists urged unilateral Western disarmament, regardless of what the Soviet Union does.

Few such unilateralists are active in the American antinuclear movement. Nor are many Americans especially concerned about missile deployment on the other side of the Atlantic. Instead, American activists have concentrated on the idea of a nuclear freeze, with talks about arms reductions to follow.

But although the president failed to recognize important differences between the European and American antinuclear movements, and although he was wrong about the origin of the freeze proposal, he was correct when he said that there has been left-wing involvement in antinuclear activity.

The Italian Communist party was the leading force behind the 1981 demonstration in Rome. In Britain, one antinuclear leader is E. P. Thompson, a former — though not current — member of the Communist party there. Spain's President Felipe González, who is sympathetic to the antinuclear cause, is a Socialist.

Many of the young Europeans who march in the streets to protest the nuclear arms race are also Communists or Socialists. Others are members of such major left-wing political groups as Britain's Labour party or West Germany's Social Democratic party. In addition, the Communist parties of several countries contribute funds to support the antinuclear movement in Europe.

But Communists are far from being the only ones involved in the European antinuclear movement. In making his charges, President Reagan ignored the fact that there are other, much more important, forces at work in it.

Nearly all the leaders of the movement in Western Europe deny that they are acting on orders from Moscow, and there seems to be no reason not to believe them. Most of their funds come not from Communist organizations but from individuals. They also receive contributions from state and local agencies. These agencies represent governments that have been freely and democratically elected.

Some European antinuclear leaders may be Communists, but many others are not. One of the two major activists in England is a former Communist, but the other is Monsignor Bruce Kent, a Roman Catholic priest. An Italian Roman Catholic group, the Italian Christian Workers' Association, organized large antinuclear demonstrations in Italy in 1983.

Nor are all European left-wingers against the nuclear arms race. In 1981, the Socialist president of France, François Mitterand, was strongly advocating increased nuclear arsenals. What's more, many antinuclear Europeans are also anti-Soviet. They urge NATO to get rid of its nuclear weapons — but to build up its conventional forces at the same time. A strong conventional army is necessary, they say, to protect the West against a possible Soviet attack.

It is true that many European demonstrators have expressed anti-American feelings. But many have expressed anti-Soviet feelings as well. "Ni Pershing ni SS-20" — Neither Pershing nor SS-20 — is a popular slogan. Most European activists are pushing for eventual disarmament by both sides. They know they can be wiped out as easily by a warhead from an SS-20 as by one from a cruise missile. "It is the same to us whether the missiles come from the east or from the west," President González of Spain pointed out.

In the United States, there is even less evidence of left-wing activity in the antinuclear movement. Alarmed by President Reagan's charges, a committee of Congress began looking into the matter. Members of the House Select Committee on Intelligence listened to the testimony of expert witnesses from the Central Intelligence Agency and the Federal Bureau of Investigation. Then they prepared a 337-page report. However, the chairman of the committee, Representative Edward Boland of Massachusetts, needed only a few words to summarize its findings. "Soviet agents have had no significant influence on the nuclear freeze movement," he noted. "The bottom line is that the hearings provide no evidence that the Soviets direct, manage, or manipulate the nuclear freeze movement."

Moscow did not start the antinuclear movement, either in this country or in Europe. Still, President Reagan was not wrong in thinking that the Soviet Union seeks to benefit from that movement. Soviet leaders are delighted by antinuclear activity, especially in Europe. They believe it may weaken NATO.

Suppose European activists continue to press their leaders to reject new American weapons, not just Pershing II's and cruise missiles, but other nuclear arms that may be offered to them in the future. Eventually, those leaders may start bickering with one another, and quarreling with the United States. The dissension might spread to include NATO military commanders. If NATO leaders cannot agree, NATO's fighting strength will diminish. Europe could become more vulnerable to Soviet advances than it has been since the end of World War II. Obviously, it is to the Soviet Union's advantage to encourage the European disarmament movement, and Soviet leaders do just that.

This galls many in the United States and Western Europe, particularly when they consider how Communist governments act toward antinuclear activists inside their own borders. In East Germany, young people were forced to stop wearing their antinuclear symbol in public. The three hundred Scandinavian women permitted to protest the arms race inside the Soviet Union in 1982 were carefully watched by Soviet police. The route of their march was changed at the last minute so few Soviet citizens would see them. Only signs and slogans that had been approved ahead of time by the Soviet government appeared on the placards they carried.

Soviet authorities treat Soviet activists far more harshly. On June 4, 1982, a week before this nation's largest-ever antinuclear demonstration began in New York City, eleven Russians announced they had formed an antinuclear movement of their own. Two days after the New York protest, all eleven were arrested and taken off to a Moscow jail. Their leader was placed in a psychiatric hospital and forced to take depressant drugs. According to his wife, he was threatened with electric shock "treatments."

It's an ugly fact that Soviet leaders do not allow even the smallest dissent in their own country, while applauding huge demonstrations elsewhere that threaten to crack the NATO alliance. But this is just one of many ugly facts about the Soviet Union, which is a totalitarian nation.

The United States and the countries of Western Europe, on the other hand, are democracies. Citizens of these nations are free to speak out and express their points of view, even if those points of view are different from official government points of view. And they must be free to continue to do so without being accused of giving "aid and comfort to the enemy," or "carrying water" for the Soviet Union.

If a democratic government discourages protest, it is not acting in the best spirit of democracy. That's why many Americans were shocked and indignant when people like President Reagan and Senator Denton tried to cast doubt on the patriotism and good sense of antinuclear activists here and abroad. "The president is hypocritical when he argues for increased military spending to help 'defend democracy,' while at the same time he undermines our democratic right to public protest," said Leslie Cragin, one of the organizers of the 1982 New York antinuclear demonstration.

Most Americans agreed. They did not believe that there was anything sinister or treasonable about the antinuclear movement. But some of them had other criticisms to make, or questions to ask, about some of the movement's goals. Most of the criticisms and questions concerned a possible threat to deterrence.

7.   What About Deterrence?

Deterrence, as nearly everyone agrees, is an extremely unattractive idea. Mutual Assured Destruction is indeed MAD. To the Conference of American Bishops, deterrence can be vengeful, immoral, and unchristian. It is a doctrine that requires a nation to acquiesce in the possible killing of millions of its people. Yet in a world that has uncovered the secrets of the atom, deterrence also seems essential.

That is because, from now on, nuclear war will always be possible. That would still be true if all the nations of the world agreed to get rid of their nuclear arms and halt every bit of military nuclear research tomorrow. Even if that happened — which is highly unlikely — nuclear knowledge would remain. That knowledge could always be turned into a new weapon.

One weapon might be enough. The United States won the world's first — so far, the world's only — nuclear war with just two bombs.

Would that nuclear war have taken place if Japan

had also possessed two nuclear weapons in 1945? Almost certainly not. Only because Japan lacked a nuclear deterrent did the United States feel safe in using its weapons.

So far, deterrence is the only reliable way the world has found to keep the nuclear peace. Deterrence must also be the basis of any effort to halt the arms race or slow it down. Unfortunately, a number of people contend, some of the ideas put forward by antinuclear activists threaten to upset deterrence.

For example, consider the European antinuclear movement that seeks to prevent deployment of new American missiles. Its critics say that if it succeeds, deterrence will crumble in Europe.

To see why, look at Europe from their point of view. The Soviet Union launches an SS-20 attack against targets in the West. How does NATO respond?

Without the new missiles, the argument goes, not very effectively. NATO's bomber fleet is old, no match for the air defenses around Warsaw Pact cities and military bases. NATO wouldn't be able to use its battlefield tactical nuclear weapons against far-off invading forces. The range of tactical weapons is so short that they would fall on NATO positions instead of Pact ones. Conventional weapons would not be much use against SS-20s and other powerful intermediate-range nuclear weapons.

So the only answer for NATO would be to strike back at the Soviets with U.S. ICBMs and SLBMs.

But would the United States actually go through with an attack on the Soviet Union in defense of Europe? If it did, the Soviets would almost certainly retaliate — against the American mainland. The United States would find itself engaged in an all-out nuclear war — just because it had tried to defend its Western European allies.

Some European leaders doubted that the United States would be willing to make such a sacrifice. More likely, they thought, this country would sit back and let the Soviet Union do what it wanted in Europe. For European leaders, this represented a "worst-case scenario."

Of course, the worst-case scenario might never come to pass. Probably the United States would go to the defense of NATO. But as long as a shadow of a doubt remained, Western European leaders thought, they must assume that the worst would happen. They must assume that the Soviet Union will take the gamble, that Soviet leaders will figure it is worth taking the chance that they can get away with conquering Western Europe.

If the Soviet Union were to figure that way, there would be no nuclear deterrent in Europe. Maybe the Soviet Union won't figure that way. But to many in NATO, the risk seemed too great to run. To avoid the risk, the United States must match the Soviets weapon for weapon — Pershing II's and cruises for SS-20s, the next generation of American weapons for the next generation of Soviet weapons, and so on.

With the newest and best weapons on hand, nuclear deterrence holds. The new weapons will easily penetrate Pact air defenses. As intermediate-range weapons, they will have no trouble reaching their proper targets. More important, they will be under the command of West European military leaders. They could be used without involving the United States. Europe could resist a Soviet attack without engulfing the world in a nuclear holocaust.

Is deployment of new missiles in Europe — not just Pershings and cruises, but other missiles that will be developed in the future — really essential to deterrence? Antinuclear activists do not believe so.

For one thing, they wonder why the Soviets, or anyone else, should assume that the United States would not go to the defense of Western Europe. There is no reason for anyone to think that this country would not honor its treaty obligations, they say. Deterrence holds in Europe because the United States wants it to hold.

It also holds because both sides already have more than enough nuclear warheads to guarantee Mutual Assured Destruction. Each could wipe out the other's population many times over. Adding new weapons simply is not necessary. All that deterrence requires is enough weapons for MAD. It does not require more than enough.

Antinuclear activists also question the notion that NATO could use Pershing II's or cruises against Pact targets without involving the United States directly. No matter who gave the order to fire the weapons, the Soviets would know where they came from in the first place. Retaliation against the United States seems a likely possibility in this case, too.

The question of deterrence is also at the root of the argument over a policy of no first use of nuclear weapons in Europe. Such a policy calls for NATO to promise never to be the first to launch a nuclear strike. The minute this idea became public, critics charged that it would make nuclear war more, not less, likely.

Ever since it was formed in 1949, NATO has relied upon a policy of first use of nuclear weapons if they are needed to repel a conventional Soviet attack. And since 1949, there has been no war in Europe. Deterrence has worked. Soviet leaders have not dared attack the West, defenders of first use say, because they know that doing so will unleash the full horror of nuclear war.

Furthermore, the first-use policy has kept the peace at a remarkably low cost for the West. Nuclear weapons are terrifically expensive to develop and build, but an equally effective conventional force would cost even more. A conventional army needs hundreds of thousands of soldiers who must be trained, clothed, fed, and paid. Tanks, artillery, and other conventional equipment must be constantly modernized and maintained in peak condition. All that takes a lot of money.

A nuclear warhead, however, doesn't need clothes or food. It doesn't need training, and requires only a minimum of upkeep. For what it costs to keep a conventional army in top fighting condition, a country can have an overpowering nuclear force. "More bang for the buck," was the way President Dwight Eisenhower — formerly General Eisenhower — put it in the 1950s.

More bang for the buck is what NATO and the United States depend on in Europe. They have a large nuclear force and a relatively small conventional one. By contrast, the Soviet Union has a large conventional army. NATO must remain willing to use its nuclear weapons against the conventional Soviet force, critics of no first use say. Not doing so might make Europe safe for conventional war.

"Safe for conventional war" is an odd phrase, but it's easy to see what those who use it mean. If the Soviets do not have to fear NATO's nuclear force, they might be tempted to go ahead with a conventional attack. Since the Soviet Union has a much stronger conventional force than NATO does, that attack might well succeed. Within days of a conventional Soviet attack, Western Europe might stand at the brink of defeat.

Then, at the last desperate moment, NATO would have to use its nuclear weapons after all, despite having promised not to do so. (Even the four men who proposed no first use conceded that this was a possibility.) That would mean the worst of both worlds. By pledging no first use, NATO would have helped prod the Soviets into starting a conventional war. Then, on the edge of losing that war, NATO would turn it into a nuclear war after all. In the view of many, it is far better for the Soviets to know, right from the start, that any strong conventional attack will lead straight to nuclear war.

The four who proposed the no-first-use policy had answers for such arguments. They did not agree that no first use would upset deterrence. For example, they recommended that NATO beef up its conventional force to approach the Soviets' strength. They reasoned that if the Soviets know for sure that a strong conventional attack on their part would be met by an equally strong conventional counterattack by NATO, they will not start a war. Conventional deterrence works, too, they pointed out. The four former officials were aware that upping NATO's conventional forces would be more expensive — in dollars — than continuing to rely on nuclear weaponry. But reliance on nuclear force is expensive in its own way. The cost of a nuclear war could be global destruction.

People argue that no first use would bolster the NATO deterrent in other ways. One member of the West German Bundestag suggested that no first use would make Europe safer by reducing the risk of nuclear war. In addition, it would make it clear that the United States is seriously trying to avoid fighting a nuclear war on European soil. This would reassure antinuclear Europeans who fear that the United States is planning to wage a "winnable" nuclear war in Europe. Such reassurance would be good for the United States in Europe. It might help heal some of the cracks in the NATO alliance — cracks that the Soviet Union was so happy to see appearing in the early 1980s.

Finally, defenders of no first use regard it as a logical extension of deterrence. The purpose of deterrence is to avoid war. Those who believe deterrence works say a nation needs nuclear weapons in order not to have to use them. With no first use, NATO would still have its nuclear weapons, but would promise not to use them first. No first use, like deterrence itself, is a way of saying, "We have nuclear weapons, but we promise not to use them unless you use yours. Then you'll wish you never had." No first use *is* deterrence, its defenders say.

Deterrence was also at issue in the pastoral letter debated by America's Roman Catholic bishops in November 1982, and formally adopted by them on May 3, 1983. In this case, it was the bishops themselves who raised the issue by condemning deterrence as immoral.

Some of the bishops, as well as some government officials, attacked that condemnation sharply. Deterrence is perfectly moral, they said, because deterrence is not a matter of revenge. The point of deterrence is to make nuclear war utterly unattractive to both sides. Only that way can war be avoided. Deterrence is the shield that stands between the earth and nuclear annihilation. That makes it moral. The Church's attack on a deterrence that keeps the nuclear peace was ignorant and irresponsible, critics said.

However, these critics overlooked the fact that the bishops did not denounce deterrence when it is used as a shield against war. In their eyes, though, that is not how deterrence is being used today. Instead, it has become the fuel for an ever-accelerating arms race.

It is in the name of deterrence that each new weapon system is designed and built. It is in the name of deterrence that NATO has refused even to consider the idea of no first use, and that the United States agreed to place new missiles in Europe. It is in the name of deterrence that American and Soviet military leaders target civilian populations as they plan for "winnable" nuclear wars.

It was this kind of deterrence that the American bishops condemned. Deterrence as a basis for arms negotiations, on the other hand, appeared morally acceptable to them. And their letter called for such negotiations — negotiations for a "bilateral verifiable agreement to halt the testing, production, and deployment of new strategic systems." In other words, a freeze.

8. What About a Freeze?

The beauty of a nuclear freeze, its advocates say, is that it would preserve deterrence while allowing for nuclear arms reductions.

One danger of a freeze, its opponents say, is that it would destroy deterrence and make the Soviets feel they have nothing to gain by negotiating arms reductions.

The argument is between those who believed the Soviet Union and the United States were at parity in the early 1980s and those who said that the Soviet Union had gotten far ahead in the arms race.

President Reagan took the latter view. His charge that President Carter had opened a "window of vulnerability" to the Soviets had helped him win the 1980 election. Once in office, he continued to maintain that the Soviets had achieved "a definite margin of superiority" over the United States.

Some people agreed with the president. General John W. Vessey, chairman of the U.S. Joint Chiefs of Staff, certainly seemed to. The Soviet Union has more ICBMs, and more powerful ICBMs, than the United States has, he informed the Senate Armed Services Committee in 1982. "In that sense, they are superior to us," he testified.

Edward Teller, the Manhattan Project scientist and "father of the hydrogen bomb," also thought the president was right. He urged United States military planners to go ahead with sophisticated new missiles and defense systems. These will place the United States far ahead of the Soviet Union in the arms race and make America safer, Teller said. Then, and only then, should this country consider negotiating with the Soviets. (Teller, of course, ignored the fact that if the United States goes ahead with an ABM system, it may well be violating the terms of SALT I.)

Secretary of Defense Caspar Weinberger agreed with the president, too, and he expressed concern about what a freeze might do to deterrence. "We think the truth is that a nuclear freeze will weaken the deterrent forces that we have to rely on to prevent war," he told Americans. He meant that with the United States behind in the arms race, a freeze would "lock" this country into an inferior position. Parity would be destroyed, the deterrent gone. Then the Soviet Union, having won permanent superiority, would never agree to cut its nuclear arsenal.

So the United States could not possibly offer the

Soviet Union a nuclear freeze. The right course for this country, President Reagan and his advisers said, was to complete the massive weapons buildup already planned for the mid-1980s. Then we can think about a freeze.

Arm first, then consider ways to disarm . . . That has a familiar ring. Probably someone said it in the Kremlin before the Soviets went ahead with the SS-20. No doubt people said it in the White House in the days of the "bomber gap" and the "missile gap." We know that Teller himself said it in 1949, when he argued in favor of building the H-bomb. This weapon, he assured the United States military, would put the United States far ahead of the Soviet Union for years and years to come.

Teller was wrong in 1949. Many thought he was just as wrong in 1982. The H-bomb didn't solve the problem of the arms race. ICBMs didn't. The Trident and the Pershing I haven't. Pershing II's and cruise missiles won't. Neither will the MX, nor the neutron bomb, nor any other weapon that may be developed in the future.

Each new weapon the United States deploys, people in the antinuclear movement say, accomplishes just one thing. It forces the Soviet Union to build and deploy a new weapon to match.

Anyway, was the United States truly in a position

where it had to strive desperately to catch up with Soviet armaments? In 1981, the Department of Defense reported that the United States and the Soviet Union were at approximate nuclear parity. When General Vessey testified in Congress, he revealed that he actually concurred with that assessment. One senator asked him if he really thought the United States were dangerously far behind the Soviet Union in nuclear arms. "Overall, would I trade?" the general responded. "Not on your life."

But parity isn't the whole point, freeze opponents answered. Even assuming that the United States is not behind the Soviet Union, a nuclear freeze that stops U.S. weapons production would be a disaster. The reason is that every new American weapon is more than just a weapon. It can also be a bargaining chip.

For instance, the antiballistic missile system was a bargaining chip for United States SALT I negotiators in 1972. American scientists had developed a workable ABM and were all set to begin setting up a defense network. That worried the Soviets. They did not want to see an ABM system, which might upset deterrence, go into operation.

"Agree to a treaty or we will deploy the ABM," American negotiators threatened. The Soviets did agree, and the two nations signed SALT I. If this country had not had its ABM bargaining chip, the argument goes, the Soviet Union might never have given in.

According to Reagan administration officials, the United States needed bargaining chips more in the 1980s than it ever had before. One chip they wanted was the MX. They planned to use the threat of deploying the MX to force the Soviets to cut back on their ICBMs. If a nuclear freeze prevented further MX testing and development, the United States would have lost a valuable negotiating tool.

Freeze advocates refused to accept this argument. Certainly, they said, the United States must have bargaining chips. But it already has plenty of them, more than it needs. Most scientific and military experts agree that American bombers, submarines, and SLBMs are far superior to Soviet models. These are adequate bargaining chips. The MX and other new weapons are not needed.

Besides, many people pointed out, bargaining chips have a way of turning into something quite different. Once, MIRVs were bargaining chips. Now they are weapons, all set and waiting to be fired. If we go ahead with the MX as a bargaining chip in an effort to reduce the numbers of older bargaining chips, what sort of weapon will we find ourselves designing twenty years from now in an attempt to negotiate away the MX bargaining chip of today?

Another objection to the freeze came from people

who feared that offering it would convince the Soviets that this country was following a policy of appeasement. That, too, could upset deterrence.

People who worried about appeasement looked to history to support their position. Appeasement means going along with someone's unreasonable demands just for the sake of peace. This was the policy practiced by several European nations toward Germany in the years before World War II.

In 1933, the Nazi leader Adolf Hitler became dictator of Germany. At once, he began preparing for war.

Fearfully, other European leaders watched German military power grow. But they did nothing to stop it, because doing something might lead to war. War was a thing most Europeans were anxious to avoid.

In 1936, Hitler invaded the Ruhr Valley, which France had taken over from Germany after World War I. France protested the invasion, but took no action that might have led to fighting.

Two years later, Hitler engineered a takeover of Austria. Again, other leaders did nothing. Peace was too precious to risk.

Within six months, Hitler was on the move again. German troops marched into Czechoslovakia. At first, British and French leaders reacted angrily. But after a conference with Hitler in Munich, Germany, they agreed to let him keep the territory he had seized.

Encouraged by the continued appeasement, Hitler tried again. In the fall of 1939, he invaded Poland. This time, Britain, France, and their allies realized they could stand by no longer. World War II began.

World War III could begin in the same way, some people believe. The Soviets, like the Nazis, have an appetite for conquest. They seized several nations in Eastern Europe after World War II. In 1979, they invaded Afghanistan. Two years later, they encouraged suppression in Communist Poland. They support revolutions around the world. All this shows that the Soviets are seriously threatening to expand their power and influence.

This threat must be met with firmness, not with appeasement, these people say. Appeasement is a sign of weakness. Western appeasement will only convince Soviet leaders that the United States dare not risk nuclear war. Appeasement won't make the Soviets more inclined to talk about arms reduction and peace. It will just make them more eager for conquest.

Most people agreed with Reagan that appeasement is a bad policy. For example, the unilateral disarmament urged by some European radicals might well encourage Soviet leaders to try to expand into

Western Europe. But few believed that a freeze would amount to appeasement.

In the first place, they said, the Soviet Union in the 1980s does not resemble Germany in the 1930s. Then, Germany was an unstable nation with an unstable ruler. The country had been badly defeated in World War I, and it went through a decade of violence, revolution, and economic chaos in the 1920s. Many historians believe that Hitler was clinically insane during at least part of his life.

The Soviet Union today is more stable than Nazi Germany ever was. Its revolution took place nearly seventy years ago. Its present leaders may be dictators, but they are not insane. They are practical, calculating men, and they have every reason to believe that the United States would never permit them to conquer Western Europe without a fight that could destroy the world.

In the second place, there is a big difference between the appeasement of the 1930s and what a nuclear freeze would accomplish. The British and French leaders of fifty years ago gave Hitler what he wanted, when he wanted it. They demanded nothing in return.

A freeze — a mutual, verifiable freeze — does demand something in return. It places obligations on both sides, Soviet as well as American. If the Soviets do not live up to those obligations, the freeze ends.

That brings up another argument against the freeze. This argument says that the Soviets cannot be trusted. If they agree to a freeze, they will not stick to its terms. They will carry out secret nuclear research. They will find ways to build and stockpile new weapons. They will only pretend to destroy missiles that they have promised to get rid of.

The United States, in the meantime, will have kept its word. Americans will have frozen their research, stopped weapons production, and destroyed great numbers of missiles. Before long, deterrence will be a thing of the past. A disarmed United States will lie at the mercy of the Soviet Union.

That is nonsense, freeze advocates retort. A freeze could certainly be verified. One American who argues this way is former Navy Rear Admiral Eugene Carroll, deputy director of the Center for Defense Information.

Shortly after the Kennedy-Hatfield freeze resolution was introduced in Congress, Carroll pointed out that such a freeze would not go into effect until the two sides had agreed on verification procedures. If they could not agree, there would be no freeze. Such a freeze would be, by its very definition, verifiable.

But, critics responded, what form would verification take? The Soviet Union and the United States have never been able to agree on a way to check up on activity at each other's military bases and research stations. The Soviets rejected the Baruch Plan partly because it called for on-site nuclear inspections. They rejected other, later U.S. proposals for the same reason. One man who worked as a White House aide during the 1970s called the subject of on-site inspections "taboo" as far as the Soviet Union is concerned.

That is not true. In the past, the Soviets have been reluctant to permit on-site inspections. But as far back as the early 1960s, during negotiations on a comprehensive test ban treaty, they did agree in principle to allow three inspections a year within their borders. At that time, however, the United States would not agree to fewer than seven annual inspections, so the agreement failed. Nearly twenty years later, in 1980, negotiators for the Soviet Union, the United States, and Britain reported to the United Nations that they had broken "significant new ground" in several areas, including on-site inspections. In 1983, the Soviet Union announced it was ready to begin talks on opening some Soviet civilian nuclear plants to UN inspection teams.

On-site inspections might not even be necessary in a freeze. Right now, without them, U.S. intelligence experts have a very good idea of what various nations are doing in nuclear weaponry. Seismographs, like the ones used to record earthquakes, are used to detect underground test explosions. Above-ground tests mean increased radiation in the atmosphere, and that, too, is easily measured.

Reconnaissance is also carried on via satellite. Photographs sent back to earth reveal even small details of missiles and missile-basing sites. This has been true for years. In the 1960s, President Johnson said that if the American space program had accomplished nothing else, it had revealed precise details about Soviet armaments. "Tonight," he told a gathering in 1967, "we know how many missiles the enemy has." We will know in the future too. Satellite photography has only grown more exact since 1967.

Reconnaissance from space, monitoring of atmospheric radiation, and seismic recordings are called "national technical means of verification." They are ways of verifying arms agreements that each nation can carry out on its own, without the cooperation of the other. By themselves, national technical means would probably be adequate to ensure that the Soviets were not cheating on a freeze. Of course, a country cannot rely on national technical means to check enemy weapons planning and designing. But it is hard to see how actual inspectors could do that job much better.

Weapons planning is not the problem, anyway — testing and production are. Two former CIA officials, William Colby and Herbert Scoville, are convinced that for keeping tabs on Soviet testing and production, national technical means of verification are sufficient. For that reason, both men have endorsed a freeze. If the Soviets do eventually agree to on-site inspections as well, so much the better.

Verification would not be a problem if a freeze were adopted. A mutual freeze is not appeasement. The United States has enough bargaining chips for negotiations. America and the Soviet Union are at approximate nuclear parity, so a freeze cannot lock in American inferiority. Therefore, a freeze — a mutual, verifiable freeze — would not upset deterrence. That was the opinion of 87 percent of Americans in 1982.

But it was not the opinion of the president and members of his administration. They were determined to defeat the freeze resolution in Congress. They were also determined to press ahead with new missile deployment in Europe and with the military buildup at home.

Above all, they were determined to show the world that their plan — arm first, talk later — would do more to prevent nuclear war than any program suggested by the antinuclear movement.

9. New Negotiations

The congressional battle over the nuclear freeze began as soon as Senators Hatfield and Kennedy introduced their resolution in March 1982. Within a month, the resolution had won the backing of 24 senators and 166 members of the House of Representatives. Hearings on it were scheduled for the summer by the committee in each house that deals with foreign-relations issues.

At each set of hearings, committee members listened to both proponents and opponents of the freeze. Proponents spoke of the overwhelming dangers of the arms race and of the need to stop it at once and begin negotiations for true arms reductions. Opponents dwelt on their belief in American nuclear inferiority, and on the need to arm first and negotiate later.

At the Senate Foreign Relations Committee hearings, freeze opponents carried the day, and committee members rejected the resolution. But in the House, freeze backers were successful. The House Foreign Affairs Committee voted in favor of the resolution.

In early August, the resolution came before the full House of Representatives. House members knew that pro-freeze sentiment was strong nationwide. Two months earlier, 500,000 people had gathered in support of a freeze in New York City, and hundreds of thousands more had rallied for the same purpose in towns and cities across the country. Letters demanding a freeze were pouring in to the offices of Congress members. Throughout the summer, they became aware of growing antinuclear feeling among business and professional groups, religious organizations, scientific societies, labor unions, and prominent men and women.

Members of the House were also under heavy pressure from the other side. President Reagan was challenging the loyalty of freeze supporters. He spoke against the freeze to groups in various states, and met with and telephoned individual representatives to urge them to vote against the resolution. The president's cabinet officers, such as the secretaries of state and defense, backed up his position with arguments of their own.

The House vote came the first week in August. It was close. Two hundred and two representatives voted in favor of the resolution. Two hundred and *four* voted against it. The president had won.

But what had he won? The Kennedy-Hatfield resolution was nonbinding. Even if both houses of Congress had passed it, Congress would have had no way
of enforcing it. The president could have simply ignored the resolution after Congress sent it to him.
Nothing would have compelled him to offer it to the
Soviet Union.

To President Reagan, though, that was not the
point. He believed that by getting Congress to turn
down the freeze, he had proved to the Soviet Union
that the United States was going to act tough regardless of the pressure from the antinuclear movement.

However, the House vote did not make the antinuclear pressure go away. Feeling in the country remained strongly in favor of a freeze and against an
escalated arms race. No sooner had the Kennedy-
Hatfield resolution failed in Congress than freeze advocates began planning for the fall congressional
elections. They drew up a list of representatives
whose votes against the freeze had been important in
its defeat. Then they started campaigns to elect antinuclear candidates to take their places in Congress.

Antinuclear activists also got freeze resolutions on
the ballots in nine states, in the District of Columbia,
and in several cities and counties. When the elections
came around, on November 2, voters passed those
resolutions in eight states, in the District, and in
twelve counties and twenty-two cities. They also

elected several new antinuclear members of Congress. Altogether, in one way or another, nearly twelve million people around the country voted in favor of a nuclear freeze on election day, 1982.

That left President Reagan with a problem. He had not changed his mind about America's need to act tough with the Soviet Union. But, like any other politician, he did not want to appear utterly opposed to something that so many people all over the country clearly supported. How could he stand as a champion of ending the arms race and reducing nuclear arsenals while not abandoning his military plans?

It was a problem the president had faced — and seemed to have solved — before. A year earlier, as huge antinuclear demonstrations took place across Europe, he had stood firm on Pershing II and cruise deployment. At the same time, he had offered the Soviet Union a plan to keep those missiles out of Europe.

The president called his proposal "simple, straightforward, yet historic." It had a catchy name — the "zero option," or the "zero-zero plan." Under it, the United States would drop plans to deploy Pershing II's and cruises. In return, the Soviet Union would dismantle all the intermediate-range missiles it had targeted on Western Europe. That would include 340 SS-20s as well as 250 older, less powerful, and less accurate SS-4s and SS-5s. The president suggested beginning Soviet-American talks on the zero option.

The president also offered to undertake negotiations to reduce stockpiles of long-range strategic weapons. He suggested calling such negotiations START — Strategic Arms Reduction Talks — to distinguish them from SALT.

Six months later, Reagan elaborated on his START plan. He offered to cut the United States strategic missile arsenal by one-third, if the Soviet Union would do the same. Both land-based and sea-based weapons stockpiles would be reduced, he said, until neither side had more than 5000 warheads. Of these, no more than 2500 on each side would be mounted on land-based ICBMs.

The Soviet Union agreed to begin negotiations. On June 29, 1982, talks opened in Geneva, Swtizerland. The United States and the Soviet Union each sent two separate sets of negotiators to Geneva. While one set from each country met to discuss the START proposals, the other talked about the zero option.

President Reagan's plan appeared to be working. He was still talking tough, rejecting the idea of a freeze, and going ahead with his projected arms-building program. Yet it was thanks to him that the new arms talks had begun. For a time, he appeared to be doing more to accomplish the goals of the antinuclear movement than the movement itself had been able to achieve. But that impression did not last long. Disturbing news began to be heard from Geneva.

To begin with, it was becoming clear that President Reagan's proposals were hardly as "simple" and "straightforward" as he had claimed. From the start, it was obvious that they would be unacceptable to the Soviets.

On the surface, the proposals seemed fair. The zero option would mean there would be neither American nor Soviet intermediate-range weapons in Europe. But to reach this point, the Soviet Union would have to dismantle hundreds of existing weapons. That would mean billions of Soviet dollars would go to waste. The United States, however, would only have to promise not to deploy weapons that were still in the testing and building stage. That would save billions for the United States. In addition, tests of the Pershing II were casting doubts on that missile's ability to perform as planned. The Soviets concluded that they were being asked to sacrifice expensive, workable missiles in return for nondeployment of unbuilt weapons that might not even work.

A second Soviet objection to the zero option was that this plan would not affect British and French missiles already targeted at Pact nations. In 1981, there were 162 such missiles. A third objection concerned American nuclear-armed submarines. The zero option would do nothing to reduce the number of SLBMs within striking range of the Soviet Union. The Soviets have felt threatened by these weapons since the 1960s, and it was to counter that threat that the Soviet Union built its SS-20s in the first place.

As for the one-third reduction plan, the Soviets saw that as a United States plan to wipe out the bulk of their nuclear arsenal. Over 70 percent of Soviet nuclear warheads are on ICBMs. Only about a quarter of the American nuclear force is on land-based missiles. A reduction to equal numbers on both sides would require the Soviet Union to destroy 5000 warheads. The United States would get to *add* 350 warheads to its ICBM aresenal. Simultaneously, reduction of SLBMs would have the United States dismantling 2500 warheads, while the Soviets would add to their stockpiles. But arms experts around the world agree that U.S. subs and SLBMs are so far superior to those of the Soviet Union that this would not damage U.S. military strength as much as destroying 5000 ICBMs would hurt the Soviet Union.

Many people thought that President Reagan and his advisers must have known that the one-third plan and the zero option would be completely unacceptable to the Soviets. In their view, the United States was offering the proposals expecting — even hoping — that the Soviets would turn them down. Then the United States would be able to go ahead with its weapons buildup while accusing the Soviet Union of wanting a continued arms race.

People will argue for years over whether that was true. But there can be no argument over the fact that the American proposals were neither simple nor straightforward. Neither, when they came, were the Soviet counterproposals.

The Soviets suggested reducing the number of their intermediate-range missiles to 300. In return, the United States would agree not to deploy any Pershing II or cruise missiles in Europe.

At the START meetings, the Soviet Union suggested reductions by one-fourth, rather than by one-third. But Soviet negotiators added that each country must be allowed to decide for itself just which weapons to get rid of.

The United States would not consider such terms. The offer of reduction by one-fourth was clearly intended to leave the overwhelmingly powerful Soviet ICBM force intact, while forcing the United States to cut into its superior SLBM arsenal.

The Soviet offer to cut its intermediate-range force to 300 was also inadequate, U.S. officials pointed out. Soviet leaders were suggesting getting rid of SS-4s and SS-5s. But these weapons were so old that they were already scheduled to be dismantled anyway. Their disposal would leave the Soviets with nearly all their modern SS-20s, each of which carries three warheads. Under the Soviet proposal, the Soviet Union would end up with 900 intermediate-range warheads in Europe, while the United States would have none. This would amount to a "West-zero, East-plus" plan.

In Geneva, one unacceptable offer had met another. "It looked like both sides were mainly posturing for world opinion," commented one former U.S. secretary of defense.

Other facts added to feelings of uneasiness regarding American sincerity about wanting to halt the arms race. In July, about a month after the Geneva talks started, President Reagan announced that the United States would no longer take part in discussions with Britain and the Soviet Union about a comprehensive test ban treaty. These discussions had been going on sporadically under six different American presidents since before the Partial Test Ban Treaty was signed in 1963. But now, President Reagan said, there was no sense in continuing them until older test ban agreements were made more "verifiable."

Was that really the reason the United States dropped out of the talks? Many American military and civilian experts are convinced that verification procedures are perfectly adequate right now. Some people thought the president was not really worried about verification at all. They suggested his motive for abandoning the negotiations was quite different.

The official Soviet news agency, TASS, accused the

president outright of using the matter of verification as "a pretext for sabotaging the talks." American news reports echoed this thought. "The most plausible motive for the decision [not to go ahead with talks] is simply that the Administration wants to keep on testing America's nuclear warheads," said an article in *Time* magazine. That conclusion seemed to be supported by the facts. The Reagan administration authorized more nuclear tests in the first eleven months of 1982 than there had been in any twelve-month period since 1970.

In September, another disquieting incident occurred. President Reagan ordered United States representatives to withdraw from the International Atomic Energy Agency (IAEA). This UN agency monitors nuclear activity around the world in an effort to slow down nuclear proliferation.

There were political reasons for the U.S. withdrawal. The IAEA had just expelled one of its other member nations, Israel. Israel is one of America's closest allies, and U.S. officials were angered by the IAEA's action. But many people believed the U.S. walkout also displayed the president's indifference to problems of proliferation.

A few months later, another event raised new suspicions about American attitudes toward halting the arms race. In January 1983, people learned that American and Soviet negotiators had come close to agreement on European missiles the previous July. But President Reagan had squashed the tentative compromise, and tried to keep word of it out of the news.

When information about the near-agreement finally did leak out, people wondered why the Reagan administration had turned it down without even a discussion. Under the compromise, the Soviet Union would have destroyed all but 75 of its SS-20s. The United States would have been allowed to counter these with 75 cruise missiles based in five NATO countries. No Pershing II's would have been deployed. Each side would have been allowed 150 medium-range bombers. The 162 British and French missiles would not have been included in the weapons count. It seemed like a fair compromise, one that might have reduced the risk of war and pleased America's NATO allies. The fact that it was rejected so curtly convinced many Europeans that the United States really was doing no more than "posturing for world opinion" at Geneva.

The Soviet Union was posturing, too. In November 1982, Soviet President Leonid Brezhnev died. His place as leader of the Soviet Union was taken by Yuri Andropov. At once, Andropov turned his attention to the arms negotiations.

In December, Andropov made a new offer to the West. In return for no new U.S. deployment, the Soviet Union would reduce its SS-20 force to 162, he said. This was a big improvement over the earlier public Soviet offer of 300. It wasn't nearly as good as the private offer of 75, but of course that had been rejected. The number 162, Andropov emphasized, was exactly the number of combined British and French missiles. If his offer were accepted, there would be an even nuclear balance in Europe.

Not so, American negotiators objected. By no means could 162 SS-20s be said to balance the 162 British and French weapons. The latter are old and outdated. Each has a single warhead, while every SS-20 carries three of the most sophisticated warheads available. The new Soviet offer, U.S. officials said, was, like the earlier one, a West-zero, East-plus plan.

Europeans, though, were not so quick to reject Andropov's offer. Antinuclear activists in Europe warned American officials to consider it carefully. True, they said, it was an offer designed to leave the Soviets at an advantage. But it was an offer — a new offer. After months without visible progress at Geneva, the Soviets were making suggestions and moving toward possible compromise. The least the United States could do, Europeans said, was to respond in a cooperative and willing spirit. America, too, must consider compromise.

European pressure on the United States was growing. It grew more over the next months, as Andropov began hinting at still another concession. Perhaps, he said, the Soviets would negotiate over numbers of warheads, instead of numbers of missiles. On May 3, 1983, Andropov made that offer official.

At first, the Soviet offer seemed to be a real step forward. So did an American concession that came at about the same time — an announcement that the Reagan administration would no longer insist on the zero option. Instead, the president said, the United States would settle for Soviet-American intermediate-range-weapon parity in Europe.

Unfortunately, most arms-control experts agreed that on closer examination the new offers left the two nations as far apart as ever at the bargaining table. The Soviet Union had agreed to negotiate over numbers of warheads — but only if British and French weapons were included in the count. President Reagan would give up the zero option — but only if the Soviets agreed to ignore British and French missiles. The Soviet Union wanted to discuss limits on medium-range bombers; the United States did not. President Reagan regarded the new Soviet offer as unacceptable, and the governments of Britain and France backed him up.

So the negotiations on European IRBMs stretched out in Geneva. By mid-1983, most observers thought it improbable that the talks, by themselves, would produce any agreement. More likely, they said, decisions about European missile basing would depend upon political circumstances. If the European antinuclear movement remained active in its opposition to cruise and Pershing II missiles, the United States might have to modify its basing plans. If, on the other hand, Western European governments stood firmly by the United States, the Soviets might back down on the issue of British and French missiles.

Experts also doubted that the Strategic Arms Reduction Talks would produce much progress. Decisions about strategic weapons, too, seemed more likely to arise from political events than from anything that might be said during formal negotiations.

For instance, there was the matter of the MX. President Reagan had asked Congress to vote funds for developing and testing the missile. He emphasized his belief that the MX was essential to American peace and security. Nevertheless, in December 1982, Congress decided to withhold $625 million in MX funding. That was a surprising defeat for the president.

One reason for it stemmed from doubts about the MX itself. The missile was supposed to be able to withstand a Soviet first strike, but many people were not at all sure it could do that. According to the Congressional Budget Office, only 10 percent of the missiles would survive such a strike. That did not seem a high percentage for a system that would cost at least $18 billion.

Another reason Congress voted against the funds had to do with the American antinuclear movement. The 1982 congressional elections had demonstrated the strength of that movement, and an increasing number of legislators hoped to compel the president to pay serious attention to it.

A few months later, in May 1983, Congress had another opportunity to show its antinuclear concern. Once more, nuclear freeze resolutions were under consideration in both houses. The Senate again turned the resolution down. But in the House of Representatives, the measure — calling for a "mutual verifiable freeze and reductions in nuclear weapons" — passed by a wide margin. The vote, 278 for, 149 against, was evidence of the shift in opinion since the House had defeated a similar resolution nine months before.

That was a second defeat for President Reagan — but it was a defeat followed almost at once by a victory. At the end of May, Congress debated new MX funding bills. This time, they passed. The vote to restore the $625 million to the missile program was 239 to 186 in the House, and 59 to 39 in the Senate.

Why? In December, the MX had seemed to be dead. How did it come to be revived only five months later — and only weeks after the House had adopted a nuclear freeze resolution?

Part of the answer lies in the fact that Congress does not like to do anything that may seem to weaken a president's hand in negotiations with another country. Reagan maintained that he absolutely had to have the MX as a bargaining chip to use against the Soviet Union. Some members of Congress were convinced by this argument. Others, although unconvinced, hesitated actually to vote against something the president claimed was vital to the country's safety.

Another part of the answer concerns two promises Reagan made to Congress just before the MX votes in May. The promises were wrung from him by senators and representatives who refused to support the MX unless the Reagan administration showed signs of taking a more active interest in arms control.

One promise went to a group of nine representatives from both political parties. It was a pledge that, once the MX had served its purpose as a bargaining chip, the United States would turn instead to so-called Midgetman missiles. Midgetman missiles would be smaller than the MX, and would carry one warhead each. They would be capable of being moved about from site to site, so Soviet targeters could never be sure where each one was. That, some people believed, would make them more likely than the MX to survive a first strike.

The president's second promise went to three senators, one Democrat and two Republicans. He agreed in writing to investigate adopting their suggestion of a nuclear "build-down." Under the build-down plan, the United States and the Soviet Union would agree to destroy two existing nuclear warheads every time they deployed one new one. This, build-down supporters said, would allow each side to reduce its nuclear stockpile while keeping its deterrent force completely up to date.

Together, the two promises were enough to satisfy a majority of the members of Congress, and to ensure their votes in favor of the MX. However, they were also enough to anger many people who questioned the president's true commitment to arms control. Skeptics pointed out that the two promises were inconsistent. The Midgetman plan calls for building many, many new missiles. Build-down requires destroying old weapons faster than new ones are built. How can a country build huge numbers of weapons while eliminating twice as many? The arithmetic just doesn't work out.

But more than arithmetic is involved. Reagan gave written promises to Congress, and Congress will be watching to see how well those promises are kept. If senators and representatives are not satisfied, they can always vote to withhold funding for future weapon building. After all, the MX is still in the planning stages. Much more money, and many more votes, will be needed to make it a reality.

If the MX does become a reality, it will be a far different weapon from the bombs that destroyed Hiroshima and Nagasaki in August 1945. Nuclear weaponry has come a long way in forty years.

So has our awareness of it. In 1945, American decisions about nuclear arms were being made in secret, by just a few military people, scientists, and politicians. Congress did not get to vote on issues like the Manhattan Project or the H-bomb. The public never got to debate them, either.

In the 1980s, the situation is different. Members of Congress can study the course of the nuclear arms race and form their own opinions about it. They have the opportunity to vote on programs like the MX. They can find ways to force even a military-minded president to make some arms-control concessions. And — if the American public wants them to — they can hold the president to those concessions.

10. Which Way for the Future?

> *Two roads diverged in a wood, and I —*
> *I took the one less traveled by,*
> *And that has made all the difference.*
> — Robert Frost, "The Road Not Taken"

Like the poet, we in the world today stand at a fork in the road. Which way will we take?

One road, the well-traveled one, beckons us seductively. It is the path along which the world has been hurtling since 1945, and it offers the sense of security and safety of the familiar. It is the road of a continued nuclear arms race.

Just ahead down the road lie Pershing II's, Trident II's, and cruise missiles. A little further along are SS-14s, which the Soviets hope will prove even more powerful and flexible than SS-20s. There is the MX, too, and the neutron bomb, the "enhanced radiation weapon."

As we journey on, we will come to weapons that will make the MX and the neutron bomb look like antiques from World War I. Already, the United States and the Soviet Union are working on these. The Soviet Union has apparently begun testing an antisatellite weapon — ASAT, for short — capable of destroying orbiting American craft. The Soviet Union is also working on an orbital bombing system that could rain nuclear warheads upon the United States from thousands of miles away from earth. According to U.S. intelligence reports, the Soviets have done considerable research into weapons armed with lasers, beams of light so narrowly focused and fast-moving that they can destroy a missile in midflight.

Futuristic American weapons lie ahead down this road, too. The United States is developing ASAT missiles to be launched from jet fighter planes, and is working on orbiting ASATs that may already outclass the Soviet models. This country is also going ahead with lasers that can cripple an enemy's command, control, and intelligence-gathering satellites.

Around the next bend in the road lurks a missile defense system that Edward Teller began urging the Reagan administration to build in 1982. Weapons in this system will be shot into space. At the heart of each will be a small nuclear bomb. If the Soviets launch a missile attack against the United States, America's orbiting bombs will be exploded. Their radiation will activate laser beams. The beams will flash to earth, destroying the attacking Soviet missiles.

Does this sound like a fantasy out of *Star Wars?* It may be. Many scientists doubt that weapons like these would ever really work. But if the world continues down the path of the arms race, such weapons will soon be tested. The United States Air Force recently established its own "Space Command." President Reagan has ordered a ground-based antisatellite system to be in operation by 1987. He wants to begin a $4 billion space weapons buildup, including hundreds of millions to be spent on laser technology alone. At the same time, America's civilian space program is being taken over more and more by the Department of Defense. The space shuttle program, for instance, began as research into the peaceful use of space. Now, the U.S. shuttle carries secret military experiments aloft.

It's no different in the Soviet Union. Civilian programs there also have military aims. Growing sums of money are being spent on space weapons research. Outer space, according to some experts in both countries, will be the battleground of the future.

How is that possible? Didn't the Outer Space Treaty of 1967, signed by the United States and the Soviet Union, forbid the launching and orbiting of "weapons of mass destruction"?

It did. However, as advocates of the new technology point out, many of the space systems they are now developing are technically not weapons of mass destruction. ASATs are designed to destroy satellites, not lives. Teller's nuclear-bomb–laser-beam project would be a defensive weapon, not an offensive one. It would be used against an enemy's attacking missiles, not against his towns and cities.

Of course, this argument misses the point. ASATs may not be weapons of mass destruction, but they would be destabilizing. If we can use them to destroy attacking missiles, we could launch our missiles first, knowing we would be able to block a Soviet second strike. The point is that every new weapon — whether offensive or defensive — fuels the arms race and makes nuclear war more likely. However, watching world leaders miss the point about the dangers of the arms race — and missing opportunities to stop it — is something we will have to continue to live with if we go on down the well-traveled road to the future.

Other ghosts from the past will haunt us. One will be self-deception.

When the first uranium bomb was dropped on Hiroshima, the world learned exactly what a nuclear weapon can do. By today's standards, that bomb was puny. If the United States builds 100 MXs, this country will have, in those few weapons alone, many thousands of times the explosive force that struck the Japanese city. Besides that, there will be all those thousands of other American weapons, the thousands of Soviet ones, and hundreds of British, French, Chinese, and Indian weapons. With just a fraction of that arsenal, people could unleash unimaginable horror upon themselves.

Almost literally unimaginable. For much as we may talk about nuclear war, or read about it, or even plan for it, few of us let ourselves truly think about it. It is too terrible an idea for most human beings to look at directly.

Talking about and planning for nuclear war without actually thinking about it requires some mental gymnastics — gymnastics that are made easier by employing a special nuclear language.

Remember the code name of the first nuclear bomb, the test bomb detonated at Alamogordo? "Trinity." To most Christians, the Trinity is a sacred concept. The bombs dropped on Hiroshima and Nagasaki were dubbed "Little Boy" and "Fat Boy." The first three of the most devastating weapons ever designed to take human life were given names that evoke holiness, youth, innocence, humor.

President Reagan named the MX "Peacekeeper." The American ASAT is known as "High Frontier." The Soviets are no less creative. They call the SS-20 "Pioneer." In the Soviet Union, the Pioneers are members of organizations like our Scout groups.

We hear other nuclear euphemisms. A nuclear war is described as a nuclear "exchange." That word brings to mind foreign students and holiday gifts. Or take "megadeath." *Mega* means one million, and one megadeath means one million dead people. It means wiping out two cities the size of Boston, or half the population of the New York City borough of Queens. But a single megadeath does not sound particularly horrible.

"Acceptable failure rate" is another useful phrase. It applies to civil defense planning. American military planners have adopted an acceptable failure rate of twenty megadeaths. Put more plainly, that means our military leaders will find it acceptable if twenty million of us perish in a nuclear war. Those same leaders also find satisfaction in the fact that the United States now has a wider variety of nuclear weapons than ever before. They refer to that variety as "a richer menu of attack options." Such language makes nuclear war sound like a Thanksgiving feast.

However, language alone cannot do the whole job of enabling people to prepare for nuclear war without thinking about it. To train military men and women in nuclear tactics, something more is needed.

That something can be a game. In 1982, the United States Navy started using computer programs that resemble video games to teach everyone from enlisted men and women to admirals how to conduct and win a war with nuclear weapons.

"We've found that it's a lot of fun," reported Navy Lieutenant Commander Bob Owen. "An awful lot of people find it just as addictive as Pac-Man." The world can only hope that those so addicted manage to retain some sense of what a real nuclear war would mean.

Some psychologists and social scientists fear that is not likely. They believe that military and civilian leaders in both the Soviet Union and the United States neither know nor understand the nature and destructiveness of the weapons at their command.

"The real horrors of nuclear war are not faced," according to Dr. Morton Deutsch of Columbia University. Dr. Deutsch calls nuclear weapons "psychologically seductive" to certain kinds of people. Such people, who have "strong power drives," are commonly found in high positions in government and in the military. To them, nuclear war may seem little more than a game, an "exchange" in which "a richer menu of attack options" may result in "megadeaths" — but not in actual destruction, suffering, and dying. People who think this way are also capable of dreaming up civil defense plans — plans in which people walk away from nuclear targets, or evacuations complete with taxes and mail delivery — that will supposedly allow a nation to survive nuclear war.

Ordinary people who lack "strong power drives" have more difficulty adjusting to the idea of nuclear war. They are afraid of it.

Most afraid of all, perhaps, are the very men and women who urge us to follow the well-traveled road of a continued arms race. That may seem odd. These are the same people who speak so eloquently of the need to display courage and determination in the face of the dangers of life in a nuclear age.

But are courage and determination really what they are talking about? Or have they confused those qualities with belligerence and stubbornness?

Think how alarmed they get at each new "enemy" deployment. Consider their nervousness as they insist on building more and more new weapons, even when many of their own military experts insist those weapons are not needed. On both sides, the drive to escalate the arms race springs less from courage than from fear.

In the 1950s, Senator Brien McMahon of Connecticut recognized that fact. "With each swing of the pendulum, the time to save civilization grows shorter," he told his fellow senators. "If we do not act, the atom will. If we do not act, we may be profaned forever by the inheritors of a ravished planet. We will be reviled, not as fools — even a fool can sense the massive danger. We will be reviled as cowards — and rightly — for only a coward can flee the

awesome facts that command us to act with forti-
tude."

George Kennan, one of those who suggested a no-
first-use policy for NATO, agrees that fear lies at the
heart of the arms race. The conviction of many that
we must constantly plan and prepare for nuclear war,
he wrote, is "a form of illness . . . some form of
subconscious despair . . . some sort of death wish
. . . a lack of faith."

A lack of faith, a lack of courage, despair — these
are what may cause the world to continue down the
road of the nuclear arms race.

What of the other road, the road less traveled by,
the road away from an escalating arms race and toward the genuine control of nuclear weapons? What
lies ahead if we decide to follow it?

No one knows, and that is why it is so difficult to
take the first step along it. But we have some ideas
about what a first step might be. It could be a nuclear freeze, or serious negotiations on a comprehensive test ban. It might be a NATO policy of no first
use, or the ratification of SALT II.

If we are to travel the road of arms control, we
will have to leave behind our ghostly companions of
the past. Suspicion and hostility will have to go, as
will name-calling and exaggerated accusations by
each side against the other. Both sides will have to
abandon the blatant propaganda and posturing that

have hampered nuclear arms negotiations from the beginning. We will have to give up the self-deceptions we use to conceal from ourselves the true horrors of nuclear war.

Which path will the world follow? Arms race? Or arms control? To many people, the old familiar road seems best, dark as it is. We know, or think we know, its dangers.

But isn't knowing those dangers — and the ultimate danger that lies at the journey's end — enough to make us choose the road less traveled by?

Glossary

Antiballistic missile (ABM) — system designed to destroy incoming enemy missiles before they can do any damage.

Antisatellite weapon (ASAT) — weapon designed to be launched into space to destroy satellites of enemy nations.

Atomic bomb (A-bomb) — nuclear fission weapon fueled by uranium or plutonium.

Counterforce capability — the ability to destroy enemy military forces.

Deterrence — the theory that nations can avoid nuclear war by threatening to meet any nuclear aggression with a devastating counterattack.

Fallout — radioactive particles, carried into the atmosphere after a nuclear explosion, which later fall back to earth.

First-strike capability — the ability to make a pre-emptive strike — the first nuclear attack in a war.

Fission — nuclear reaction in which atoms of a heavy material are split — fissioned — apart.

Fusion — nuclear reaction in which atoms of a light material are joined — fused — together.

Ground zero — the point on the earth's surface at which, or directly above which, a nuclear weapon is detonated.

Hydrogen bomb (H-bomb) — nuclear fission-fusion weapon fueled by hydrogen.

Intercontinental ballistic missile (ICBM) — nuclear weapon with a range of up to 3000 miles.

Intermediate-range ballistic missile (IRBM) — nuclear weapon with a range of up to 1200 miles.

Megaton — one million tons. Nuclear explosions are measured in terms of equivalent tons of TNT. A one-megaton bomb produces the explosive force of one million tons of TNT.

Multiple independently targetable reentry vehicles (MIRVs) — reentry vehicles carried by a ballistic missile, each of which can be directed to a separate, distinct target.

Multiple reentry vehicles (MRVs) — reentry vehicles carried by a ballistic missile that fall to earth separately, but not directed to specific targets.

Mutual Assured Destruction (MAD) — the theory that nations can avoid nuclear conflict by promising to destroy each other in any such conflict.

Neutron bomb (enhanced radiation weapon) — nuclear weapon whose intense fusion reaction enables it to release more energy as radiation than as blast.

Non-Proliferation Treaty (NPT) — signed in 1973, attempts to limit the spread of nuclear weapons to nations that do not already have them.

North Atlantic Treaty Organization (NATO) — set up in

1949, an alliance of the United States, Canada, Iceland, and thirteen nations of Western Europe.

Outer Space Treaty — signed in 1967, forbids putting nuclear weapons in space.

Partial Test Ban Treaty — signed in 1963, attempts to limit nuclear weapons testing in the atmosphere, in outer space, and in the ocean.

Sea Bed Treaty — signed in 1972, forbids the placing of nuclear weapons on the ocean floor.

Strategic Arms Limitations Treaties (SALT I and SALT II) — treaties designed to set limits on strategic weapons and defense systems. SALT I was signed in 1972 and ratified by the United States Senate; SALT II was signed in 1979 but not ratified.

Submarine-launched ballistic missiles (SLBMs) — nuclear weapons designed to be fired from submarines.

Warsaw Pact — set up in 1955, an alliance of the Union of Soviet Socialist Republics and six nations of Eastern Europe.

Bibliography

Here is a list of books that offer more information about nuclear weapons, the nuclear arms race, and nuclear war. Two of them tell about life in Hiroshima during and after the nuclear war in Japan. Three others — all fiction — speculate about what life might be like for those who survive an all-out nuclear war in the future.

Barnet, Richard J. *Who Wants Disarmament?* Boston: Beacon Press, 1960.

Briggs, Raymond. *When the Wind Blows.* New York: Schocken, 1982.

Dougherty, James E. *How to Think About Arms Control and Disarmament.* New York: Crane, Russak & Company, 1973.

Ground Zero, Inc. *Nuclear War: What's In It for You?* New York: Simon & Schuster, 1982.

Hersey, John. *Hiroshima.* New York: Alfred A. Knopf, 1946.

Kennan, George F. *The Nuclear Delusion: Soviet-American Relations in the Atomic Age.* New York: Pantheon Books, 1982.

Maruki, Toshi. *Hiroshima No Pika*. New York: Lothrop, Lee & Shepard, 1982.

Miller, Walter M., Jr. *A Canticle for Leibowitz*. New York: Bantam, 1976.

Myrdal, Alva. *The Game of Disarmament: How the United States and Russia Run the Arms Race*. New York: Pantheon Books, 1976.

Roberts, Chalmers M. *The Nuclear Years: The Arms Race and Arms Control*. New York: Praeger, 1970.

Russell, Bertrand. *Common Sense and Nuclear Warfare*. New York: Simon & Schuster, 1959.

Schell, Jonathan. *The Fate of the Earth*. New York: Alfred A. Knopf, 1982.

Schweitzer, Albert. *Peace or Atomic War?* New York: Henry Holt and Company, 1958.

Shute, Nevil. *On the Beach*. New York: Ballantine, 1978.

Index

327.1
WEI

Weiss, Ann E.

The nuclear arms race : can we survive it?

$9.86

DATE DUE	BORROWER'S NAME	ROOM NO.
DEC __	David Adelman	
APR 1	James Ricely	
MAR 1 8	David Savage	
DEC		

327.1
WEI

Weiss, Ann E.

The nuclear arms
race : can we
survive it?

WATERLOO HIGH SCHOOL LIBRARY
1464 INDUSTRY RD, ATWATER OHIO

472566 00990A